Sunset

■BEAUTIFUL THINGS TO MAKE FOR
baby

🐤 **Knitting**   🐤 **Sewing**   🐤 **Crochet**   🐤 **Embroidery**

SUNSET PUBLISHING CORPORATION ■ MENLO PARK, CALIFORNIA

The arrival of a new baby is the most exciting news! And what is the first thing we "crafty" people do when we hear of a new baby expected by a family member or friend? We rush straight to our box of favorite patterns to find a special gift to make. Well it's all here — knitting, sewing, crochet and embroidery. There are traditional and contemporary styles to suit every baby and every crafter.

We've included designs for babies of all ages from birth to about one year. Each one is pictured in a full-color photo and accompanied by easy-to-follow instructions. Follow our special hints and tips to ensure a perfect result for that very special new arrival.

ALL ABOUT SIZES

All sewn garments are given in one of two sizes:

0 to 6 months

6 to 12 months

All knitted and crocheted items are sized by actual measurements specified in inches.

All of our patterns are graded by skill level. Just look for the hearts at the beginning of each pattern.

♥ Easy: Achievable by anyone

♥ ♥ Average: For those with some experience

♥ ♥ ♥ Challenging: For more experienced crafters

91239

Published in 1993 by Sunset Publishing Corporation, Menlo Park, CA 94025 by arrangement with J.B. Fairfax Press Pty Limited

First Sunset Printing August 1993

Editor, Sunset Books: Elizabeth L. Hogan

Cover copyright © 1993 Sunset Publishing Corporation; Design by Nina Bookbinder Design; Photography by Bill Zemanek Photography; Photo Syling by Shelley Pennington

Library of Congress Catalog Card Number: 93-84315
ISBN 0-376-04295-8
Lithographed in the United States

J.B. FAIRFAX PRESS PTY LIMITED
EDITORIAL
Craft Editor: Tonia Todman
Managing Editor: Judy Poulos
Editor: Marian Broderick
Editorial Co-ordinator: Margaret Kelly
Assistant Craft Editor: Sally Pereira
Sewing and craft assistance: Martina Oprey, Yvonne Deacon, Elsie Hamerlok, Natalie Wise, Ann Cavalho
Australian Editorial Coordinators: Claire Pallant, Nadia Sbisa

KNITTING DESIGN
All patterns knitted, crocheted, designed and written by Sheryl Braden; Sue Morton; Kathy Jarvis and Wyn McNamara

DESIGN AND PRODUCTION
Nadia Sbisa; Margie Mulray; Chris Hatcher

ILLUSTRATIONS
Greg Gaul

PHOTOGRAPHY
Andrew Elton, Andrew Payne

Contents

Spring Baby

All the colors and freshness of spring! Here are cozy knits to wear on their own or to team with crisp cottons. See how we've spiced up a simple knitted suit with some baby-sized motifs and then repeated the same motifs on the beautiful appliquéd crib quilt. If you're a whiz with a crochet hook there's a baby afghan and matching pillows to make, colored with a touch of primroses.

CROCHETED COVERLET AND PILLOWS

TECHNIQUE: Crocheting

DIRECTIONS
MOTIF A
Make 10 for Coverlet and 2 for each Pillow. Using hook and C, ch 6. Join with sl st to form a ring.

Rnd 1: Ch 1, (3 sc, ch 4) 4 times in ring. Sl st in first ch at beg.

Rnd 2: Ch 1, sc in next sc, * sc in each of next 2 sc, sl st in next ch-4 lp, ch 9, sl st in same ch-4 lp, sc in next sc; rep from * 3 times, omitting sc in next sc in last rep, sl st in first ch at beg. Fasten off.

Rnd 3: Holding ch-9 lp to front, join B with a sl st in ch-4 sp of 1st rnd, ch 3, (dc, ch 2, 2 dc) in sp behind ch-9 lp, dc in each of next 3 sc, * holding ch-9 lp to front (2 dc, ch 2, 2 dc) in ch-4 sp of 1st rnd, dc in each of next 3 sc; rep from * to end. Sl st in 3rd ch at beg.

Rnd 4: Ch 3, dc in next dc, * 2 dc in next ch-2 sp, dc in ch-9 lp, ch 9, sl st in first of these ch, dc in ch-9 lp, 2 dc in same ch 2, dc in each of next 2 dc, ch 3, sk 3dc, dc in each of next 2 dc; rep from * omitting dc in each of next 2 dc at end of last rep, using A sl st in 3rd ch at beg.

Rnd 5: Using A, ch 3, * dc in each of next 3 dc, with ch-9 lp in front of work (2 dc, ch 2, 2 dc) around sl st at base of ch-9 of Rnd 4, dc in each of next 4 dc, working in front of ch 3 of Rnd 4, tr in each of next 3 dc of Rnd 3, dc in next dc; rep from * omitting dc in next dc at end of last rep. Sl st in 3rd ch at beg.

Rnd 6: Ch 3, * dc in each of next 5 dc, 2 dc in next ch-2 sp, dc in ch-9 lp of Rnd 4, ch-9, sl st back into first of these ch, dc in same 9 ch lp of 4th rnd, 2 dc in same ch-2 sp of Rnd 5, dc in each of next 6 dc, ch 3, sk 3 tr, dc in next dc; rep from * omitting dc in next dc at end of last rep, using Mc sl st in 3rd ch at beg.

Rnd 7: Using Mc, ch 3, * dc in each of next 7 dc, with ch-9 lp in front of work (2 dc, ch 1, 2 dc) around sl st at base of ch-9 of Rnd 6, dc in each of next 8 dc, 1 tr in each of next 3 tr of Rnd 5, dc in next dc; rep from

SIZE
Directions are given for a Coverlet about 28" x 46" (including border) and Pillows each about 12½" square (including border).

MATERIALS
Sport-Weight 3-Ply Yarn (50 gr. ball): 8 balls of main color (Mc) and 3 balls each of 3 contrasting colors (A, B, C) for coverlet; 2 balls of Mc and 1 ball each of A, B, C for two pillows: Size C crochet hook, *or any size hook to obtain gauge below*; 2 pillow forms; tapestry needle.

GAUGE
23 dc = 4"; 12 rows = 4". Be sure to check your gauge.

* omitting dc in next dc at end of last rep, sl st in 3rd ch at beg.

Rnd 8: Ch 1, * sc in each st to ch-1 corner sp, sc in ch-1 sp, ch 1, sc in ch-9 lp of Rnd 6, ch 1; rep from * to end, sl st in ch-1 at beg. Fasten off.

MOTIF B
Make 10 for Coverlet and 2 for each Pillow.

Work as for Motif A, using A in place of C, C in place of B, and B in place of A.

MOTIF C
Make 10 for Coverlet and 1 for each Pillow.

Work as for Motif A, using A in place of B, and B in place of A.

MOTIF D
Make 10 for Coverlet and 1 for each Pillow.

Work as for Motif A, using B in place of C, and C in place of B.

MOTIF E
Make 10 for Coverlet and 1 for each Pillow. Work as for Motif A, using A in place of B, C in place of A, and B in place of C.

MOTIF F
Make 10 for Coverlet and 1 for each Pillow. Work as for Motif A, using A in place of C, and C in place of A.

TO ASSEMBLE
Join motifs together as indicated in charts below. With right sides facing you sew motifs together, from the center of a corner to center of next corner, matching sts along side edges and working through back loops only.

For Pillows:
With wrong sides of Pillow front and back together, using Mc, sc around three edges, working 3 sc in each corner sc, and having a multiple of 10 plus 1 dc between corners. Insert pillow form and slipstitch opening closed.

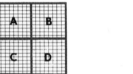

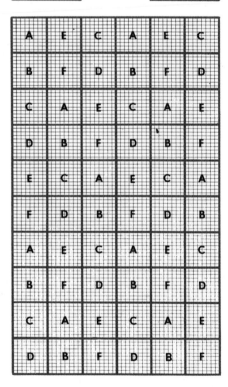

For Coverlet:
With right side facing you, using Mc, work 1 round of sc evenly around all edges of coverlet, working 3 sc in each corner sc, and having a multiple of 10 plus dc between corners. Sl st in first sc at beg. Fasten off.

BORDER FOR COVERLET AND PILLOWS:
Using Mc, beg at one corner:

Rnd 1: Ch 1, ** sc in corner sc, ch 5, sk 3 sc, * sc in each of next 7 sc, ch 5, sk 3 sc **; rep from * to next corner dc, then rep from ** to ** 3 times more. Sl st into first sc at beg.

Rnd 2: Ch 4, ** into the ch-5 lp work a "leaf" as follows: *, (yo) twice, insert hook under lp, yo, and draw up a lp, (yo, and draw through 2 lps on hook) twice*, you now have 2 lps remaining on hook; rep from * to * 2 times more, you now have 4 lps on hook, yo, and draw through 3 lps on hook, yo, and draw through rem 2 lps on hook to complete the "leaf"; all in same ch-5 lp as first "leaf" work (ch 3, 2nd "leaf", ch 5, 3rd "leaf", ch 3, 4th "leaf")**; rep from ** to ** in each ch-5 lp, skipping the sc between each lp, sl st into beg ch-4 .

Rnd 3: Ch 4; rep from ** to ** of Rnd 2 in each ch-5 lp, sl st in beg ch-4. Fasten off.

PICTURE QUILT

TECHNIQUE: Sewing

SIZE: 27 1/2" x 39 1/4"

MATERIALS
- [ ] 1 3/4 yards of 45"-wide green cotton
- [ ] 5/8 yard of 45"- wide white cotton
- [ ] 3/8 yard of 45"-wide yellow cotton
- [ ] 30" x 42" batting
- [ ] 3/4 yard of 18"-wide fusible web
- [ ] fabric scraps for appliqués

NOTE: Seam 3/8" deep with right sides pinned together.

DIRECTIONS
1 Cutting: *From green fabric,* cut a 30" x 42" quiltback, three 11"-square

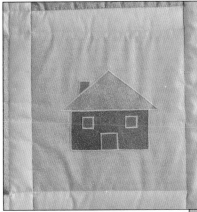

quiltblocks and four 3 1/8"-wide bindings — two 30" long and two 41" long. *From yellow fabric,* cut three 11" squares. *From white fabric,* cut four 2 1/4"-wide sashing strips 11" long and one 34 1/2" long. Also cut four 3 1/8"-wide border strips — two 35" and two 28" long.

2 Appliqué Patterns: Draw the following rectangles: a 3" x 6" house, a 3" x 8" roof, a 7" x 5" sail and a 2" x 8" boat. Fold the roof piece in half (to 3" x 4") and draw from the top end of the fold down to the open corner of the bottom edge. Cut on the drawn line. Fold the sail in half (to 3 1/2" x 5") and cut the same way. Fold the boat piece in half (to 2" x 4"), mark the bottom edge 2" from the fold and draw from that mark up to the open end of the top edge, then cut along the line. Draw a door, a chimney and a window pattern.

3 Appliqué: Pin fusible web to the wrong side of the appliqué fabric. Pin the patterns on top and cut the following through both layers: 3 each of the house, roof, sail and boat. Iron the appliqués to the quiltblocks (see picture above) and edgestitch. Then cover the edges with machine zigzag stitch. In the same way cut and stitch the windows, door and chimney.

4 Seaming: To the top and bottom edges of the 2 center quiltblocks, seam one of the 11"-long sashings. To the raw edge of each sashing, seam a quiltblock (see photo). Then seam the 34 1/2" sashing between the 2 vertical rows of blocks.

5 Border: Seam a longer border strip to each side edge of the quilt and trim its

ends flush with the quiltblocks. Seam the other border strips to the top and bottom edges; trim the ends flush with the side edges.

6 Basting: Spread out the quiltback wrong side up. On top spread the batting, with edges even. Center the quilttop, right side up, over the batting. Pin layers together near the center. With long stitches, baste through all layers from the center outward to the center of each edge, then from center to each corner. Add another basting row halfway between these rows.

7 Quilting: By hand or machine, stitch in the ditch of the white sashing seams and the inside edges of the white border. Along the outside border, baste through all layers around the quilt.

8 Finishing: Trim batting and quiltback flush with the white border edges. Seam each longer green binding to a long side edge of the quilt, with right sides together and edges even. Trim the ends flush with the quilt. Turn half the binding to the quiltback, turn under its raw edge and slipstitch. Seam the other binding strips to top and bottom edges with 1/2" of binding extending from each side. Turn in the extending ends, flush with the side edges; turn under the long edge and slipstitch. Remove the bastings.

BABY'S JUMPSUIT

TECHNIQUE: Knitting

DIRECTIONS
BACK
RIGHT LEG
** Beg at ankle, using No.1 needles and Mc cast on 25 sts.

Row 1: K 2, * p 1, k 1; rep from * to last st, k 1.

Row 2 (right side): K 1, * p 1, k 1; rep from * to end.

Rows 3-4: Rep Rows 1 and 2 once.

Rows 5-6: Using A, rep Rows 1 and 2 once.

Rows 7-9: Using Mc, rep Rows 1 and 2 once, then Row 1 once for lower band.

Row 10: (Inc in next st, rib 1) 5(2) times, inc in each of next 5(17) sts, (rib 1, inc in next st) 5(2) times — 40(46) sts.

Rows 11-28: Change to No. 3 needles. Using Mc, work 18 rows st st (k 1 row , p 1 row).

Rows 29-32: Using A, work 4 rows in garter st (k every row).
Last 22 rows form pattern.

Continue in pat until work measures 5½ (6½)" from beg, ending on wrong side. **
Keeping in pat, inc one st at end of every row 5 times, then every other row once — 46(52) sts.

Cut yarn, leave sts on a stitch holder.

LEFT LEG
Work as for Right Leg from ** to **.
Keeping in pat, inc one st at beg of every row 5 times, then every other row once — 46(52) sts.

Next Row: Work in pat across 46(52) sts, then in pat across 46(52) sts on stitch holder — 92(104) sts.

Crotch Shaping:
Keeping in pat work as follows:

Next Row: Work in pat across 44(50) sts, (work 2 tog) twice, pat across 44(50) — 90(102) sts.
Work even for 1 row.

Next Row: Work in pat across 43(49), (work 2 tog) twice, pat across 43(49).
Work even for 1 row.

Next Row: Work in pat across 42(48), (work 2 tog) twice, pat across 42(48) — 86(98) sts.

Continue to dec in this manner every other row until 78(90) sts rem, then every 4th

SIZE
Directions are given for Size 3 months. Changes for 6 months are in parentheses.

MATERIALS
Fingering-Weight Yarn (50 gr. ball): 2(3) balls of main color (Mc), 1 ball of contrasting color (A); 1 pair each No. 1 and No. 3 knitting needles, *or any size needles to obtain gauge below;* stitch holder; 5 (6) buttons; tapestry needle.

GAUGE
On No. 3 needles in stockinette stitch (st st) — 8 sts = 1"; 11 rows = 1". Be sure to check your gauge.

MEASUREMENTS

Sizes (mos.):	3	6
Body Chest:	16"	18"
Finished Measurements:		
Chest:	18"	20"
Length (under arm to ankle):		
	16¾"	18¼"
Sleeve Length:	5¼"	6"

row until 74(86) sts rem***.
Keeping in pat, work until piece measures about 16(17½)" from beg of ankle, ending with 4 rows in A. Mark each end of last row for beg of armholes. Using Mc only, work 42(46) rows in st st.

Shoulder Shaping:
Bind off 8(10) sts at beg of next 4 rows, then 8(9) sts at beg of next 2 rows. Leave rem 26(28) sts on a stitch holder.

FRONT
Work as given for Back to ***.
Work even for 1 row.

Divide for front opening:
Keeping in pat, work as follows:

Next Row: Work in pat across 34(40), bind off next 6 sts, pat across 34(40).

Work on last 34(40) sts for first side until Front measures same as Back to markers, ending with 4 rows A.

Mark beg of last row for beg of armhole.
Using Mc only, work 24(28) rows in st st.

Neck Shaping:
Bind off 5 sts at beg of next row.
Dec one st at neck edge every other row until 24(29) sts rem.
Work even for 8(6) rows.

Shoulder Shaping:
Bind off 8(10) sts at beg of next row and every other row once.

Work even for 1 row.
Bind off 8(9) sts.
Join yarn to rem sts and work to correspond with other side, marking beg of armhole at end of last row and working one row more before neck shaping.

SLEEVES
Using No. 1 needles and Mc, cast on 41(45) sts.
Work 10 rows in rib and stripes as for lower band of Back, inc 12 sts evenly across last row — 53(57) sts.
Change to No. 3 needles.
Continuing in st st, inc one st at each end of 3rd row, then every 4th row until there are 59(61) sts, then every 6th row until there are 65(71) sts.
Work even until length measures 5¼(6)" from beg, ending with a purl row.

Cap Shaping:
Bind off 8(9) sts at beg of next 6 rows.
Bind off rem 17 sts.

RIGHT FRONT BAND
Sew shoulder seams.
With right side facing, using No. 1 needles and Mc, pick up and k 73(85) sts evenly along front edge to neck shaping.
Work 3 rows in rib as for lower band of Back, beg with Row 2.
Next Row: Using A, rib 7, * yo, work 2 tog, rib 15(14); rep from * 2(3) times more, yo, work 2 tog, rib 13(12) — *4(5) buttonholes made.*
Work even for 1 row.
Using Mc, work 4 rows in rib.
Bind off loosely in rib.

LEFT FRONT BAND
Work as for Right Front Band, omitting buttonholes.

NECKBAND
With right side facing, using No. 1 needles and Mc, pick up and k 63(65) sts evenly along neck edge and side edge of front bands (including sts from stitch holder).
Work 3 rows in rib as for lower band of Back, beg with Row 2.
Next Row: Using A, rib 3, yo, work 2 tog, rib to end.
Work even for 1 row.
Using Mc, work 4 rows in rib.
Bind off loosely in rib.

FINISHING
Sew in sleeves between markers, placing center of sleeves at shoulder seams. Sew side, sleeve and leg seams. Sew front bands in place overlapping at center where sts were bound off. Sew on buttons.

GREEN KNIT CARDIGAN

TECHNIQUE: Knitting

DIRECTIONS
BACK
Using No. 1 needles, cast on 71(79,85,93) sts.
Row 1: K 2, *p 1, k 1; rep from * to last st, k 1.
Row 2: K 1, *p 1, k 1; rep from * to end.
Rep Rows 1 and 2 for lower band until band measures 1¼(1¼,1¼,1½)" from beg, ending with Row 2.
Change to No. 3 needles.
Rows 1-4: Work 4 rows in st st (k 1 row , p 1 row).
Row 5: K 5(3,6,4), *yo, sl 1, k 1, psso, k 4; rep from * to last 0(4,1,5) sts, (yo, sl 1, k 1, psso) 0(1,0,1) times, k 0 (2,1,3).
Row 6: Purl.
Row 7: K 3(1,4,2), * k 2 tog, yo, k 1, yo, sl 1, k 1, psso, k 1; rep from * to last 2(0,3,1) sts, k 2(0,3,1).
Work 5 rows in st st, beg with a purl row.
Row 13: K 2(6,3,1), * yo, sl 1, k 1, psso, k 4; rep from * to last 3(1,4,2) sts, (yo, sl 1, k 1, psso) 1(0,1,1) times, k 1(1,2,0).
Row 14: Purl.

SIZE
Directions are given for size 3 months. Changes for 6 months, 9 months and 12 months are in parentheses.

MATERIALS
Fingering-Weight Yarn (50 gr. ball): 1(1,2,3) balls; 1 pair each No. 1and No. 3 knitting needles, *or any size needles to obtain gauge below*; 8 small buttons; 4 velcro dots; tapestry needle.

GAUGE
On No. 3 needles in stockinette stitch (st st) — 8 sts = 1"; 11 rows = 1". Be sure to check your gauge.

MEASUREMENTS

Sizes (mos.):	3	6	9	12
Body Chest:	16"	18"	20"	22"
Finished Measurements:				
Chest:	17¼"	19½"	21½"	23½"
Length to back neck:				
	9"	10"	12"	13"
Sleeve Length:				
	5½"	6½"	8"	9½"

Row 15: K 3(4,1,2), (yo, sl 1, к 1, psso, к 1) 1(0,0,1) times, * k 2 tog, yo, k 1, yo, sl 1, k 1, psso, k 1; rep from * to last 5(3,0,4) sts, (k 2 tog, yo), 1(0,0,1) times, k 3(3,0,2).
Row 16: Purl.
Last 16 rows form pattern.
Work 68(80,96,108) rows in pattern.

Shoulder Shaping:
Keeping in pat, bind off 11(13,14,15) sts at beg of next 2 rows, then 12(13,14,16) sts at beg of next 2 rows.
Bind off 25(27,29,31) sts.

LEFT FRONT
Using No. 1 needles, cast on 51(57,63,69) sts.
Work in rib as for lower band of Back, until band measures 1¼(1¼,1¼,1½)" from beg, ending with Row 2 and inc 0(0,1,1) st in center of last row — 51(57,64,70) sts.
Change No. 3 needles. **
Rows 1-4: Work 4 rows in st st.
Row 5: K 5(3,6,4), * yo, sl 1, k 1, psso, k 4; rep from * to last 4(0,4,0) sts, (yo, sl 1, k 1, psso) 1(0,1,0) time, k 2(0,2,0).
Row 6: Purl.

Row 7: K 3(1,4,2), * k 2 tog, yo, k 1, yo, sl 1, k 1, psso, k 1; rep from * to last 0(2,0,2) sts, k 0(2,0,2).

Work 5 rows st st (beg with a purl row).

Row 13: K 2(6,3,1), *yo, sl 1, k 1, psso, k 4; rep from * to last 1(3,1,3) sts, (yo, sl 1, k 1, psso) 0(1,0,1) times k 1.

Row 14: Purl.

Row 15: K 3(4,1,2), (yo, sl 1, k 1, psso, k 1), 1(0,0,1) times, *k 2 tog, yo, k 1, yo, sl 1, k 1, psso, k 1; rep from * to last 3(5,3,5) sts, k 2 tog, yo, k 1, (yo, sl 1, k 1, psso), 0(1,0,1) times.

Row 16: Purl.

Last 16 rows form pattern.

Keeping in pat, dec one st at end of next and then every other row until 28(33,39,43) sts rem, then every 4th row until 23(26,28,31) sts rem.

Work even for 3(5,3,7) rows.

Shoulder Shaping:
Keeping in pat, bind off 11(13,14,15) sts at beg of next row.

Work even for 1 row.

Bind off.

RIGHT FRONT
Work as for Left Front to **.

Rows 1-4: Work 4 rows in st st.

Row 5: K 3(5,3,5), * yo, sl 1, k 1, psso, k 4; rep from * to last 0(4,1,5) sts, (yo, sl 1, k 1, psso) 0(1,0,1) times, k 0(2,1,3).

Row 6: Purl.

Row 7: K 1(3,1,3), * k 2 tog, yo, k 1, yo, sl 1, k 1, psso, k 1; rep from * to last 2(0,3,1)

sts, k 2(0,3,1).

Work 5 rows in st st, beg with a purl row.

Row 13: K 6(2,6,2), *yo, sl 1, k 1, psso, k 4; rep from * to last 3(1,4,2) sts, (yo, sl 1, k 1, psso) 1(0,1,1) times, k 1(1,2,0).

Row 14: Purl.

Row 15: (K 1, yo, sl 1, k 1, psso, k 1) 1,(0,1,0) times, * k 2 tog, yo, k 1, yo, sl 1, k 1, psso, k 1; rep from * to last 5(3,0,4) sts, (k 2 tog, yo) 1(0,0,1) times, k 3(3,0,2).

Row 16: Purl.

Last 16 rows form pattern.

Continuing in pat, work to correspond with Left Front, reversing shaping and working 1 row more before shoulder shaping.

SLEEVES
Using No. 1 needles, cast on 41(41,43,43) sts.

Work in rib as for lower band of Back, until band measures 1¼" from beg, ending with Row 2 and inc 8(8,6,6) sts evenly across last row — 49 sts.

Change to No. 3 needles.

Work in pat as for Back, following directions as given for "2nd size." **At the same time** inc one st at each end of 7th row and then every 4th(4th,2nd,4th) row until there are 59(65,53,75) sts, then in every 6th(6th,4th,6th) row until there are 61(67,73,79) sts.

Work even until length measures 5½ (6½,8,9½)" from beg, ending with a purl row.

Cap Shaping:
Keeping in pat, bind off 5(5,6,6) sts at beg of next 8 rows.

Bind off rem sts.

FRONT BAND
Sew shoulder seams.

Using No. 1 needles, cast on 9 sts.

Row 1: K 2,(p 1,k 1) 3 times, k 1.

Row 2: K 1,(p 1,k 1) 4 times.

Rep Rows 1 and 2 once.

Row 5: Rib 3, yo, k 2 tog, rib 4.

Work 7 rows in rib.

Rep last 8 rows twice, then 5th row once — *4 buttonholes made.*

Work even in rib until band is long enough to fit (slightly stretched) evenly along fronts and across back of neck.

Bind off loosely in rib.

FINISHING

Sew in sleeves, placing center of sleeves at shoulder seams. Sew side and sleeve seams. Sew front band in position, placing buttonholes at right front. Overlap fronts, sew on buttons to correspond with buttonholes. Sew 4 more buttons onto Right Front, matching buttons. Sew velcro dots underneath buttons to fasten.

GREEN FLORAL PANTS

TECHNIQUE: Sewing

SIZE: 6 to 12 months

MATERIALS
☐ ⅝ yard 45"-wide fabric
☐ ⅝ yard ½"-wide elastic
☐ tracing paper and pencil
☐ sewing thread to match fabric

NOTE: Seam ⅜" deep with the pieces pinned right sides together. To "cut a pair," pin the pattern to double fabric.

DIRECTIONS
Pattern outline — — — — — — —
1 Pattern: Trace pattern 20 (see pullout sheet). You can add a cuff if you lengthen this pattern by the distance between its lower edge and the drawn cuffline. This added length makes a facing, so you can turn up the pant leg.

2 Crotch Seam: Pin the two pieces right sides together with backs matching. Stitch

Green Knit Cardigan, Green Floral Pants, Picture Knit Pullover and Pants

the back crotch seam, then the front crotch. Press seams open.

3 Inner Leg Seams: Fold the pants so the crotch seams are centered and matching (right sides together). Pin the two inner leg seams and stitch the whole seam from one leg edge to the other. Press seam open.

4 Lower Edge: Fold up the facing, turn under 1/4" and hem it securely.

5 Waist Edge: Overcast the top edge with zigzag stitch if you have it. Turn it 3/4" to the inside and press. Stitch the finished edge, leaving a small opening. Insert elastic through the casing, adjust its length to fit and stitch the ends securely together.

PICTURE KNIT PULLOVER AND PANTS

TECHNIQUE: Knitting

NOTE: When changing colors, pick up new color from under the color being used, twisting yarns on wrong side of work to prevent holes. Carry color not in use loosely across wrong side of work, being careful to maintain gauge. Use a separate bobbin for each color change.

DIRECTIONS
PULLOVER
BACK
Using No. 1 needles and C, cast on 75(83,91) sts.

Row 1: K 2, * p 1, k 1; rep from * to last st, k 1.

Row 2: K 1, * p 1, k 1; rep from * to end. Rep Rows 1 and 2 until lower band measures 3/4" from beg, ending with Row 2, inc one st at end of last row — 76(84,92) sts. Change to No. 3 needles.

Work Rows 1 to 73 of chart at sizes indicated.

Next Row: P 38(42,46) Mc, p 38(42,46) A.

Next Row: K 38(42,46) A, k 38(42,46) Mc. Last 2 rows form pat. **

Work 19(23,31) rows in pat.

Back Neck Shaping:
Keeping in pat, work as follows:

Next Row: Work in pat across 22(24,27), turn.

Dec one st at neck edge in every row until

SIZE
Directions are given for size 3 months. Changes for 6 months and 9 months are in parentheses.

MATERIALS
Fingering-Weight Yarn (50 gr. ball): 1(1,2) balls of pink (Mc), 1(1,2) balls of blue (A), 1 ball each of yellow (B) and green (C) for Pullover; 2(2,3) balls of Mc, 1 ball each of A, B and C for Pants; 1 pair each No. 1 and No. 3 knitting needles, *or any size needles to obtain gauge below*; 2 stitch holders; bobbins; 3 buttons for Pullover; elastic for Pants.

GAUGE
On No. 3 needles in stockinette stitch (st st) — 8 sts = 1"; 11 rows = 1". Be sure to check your gauge.

MEASUREMENTS

Sizes (mos.):	3	6	9
Body Chest:	16"	18"	20"
Finished Measurements:			
Chest:	18"	20"	22"
Length to back neck:			
	10"	10½"	11¼"
Sleeve Length:			
	6"	7"	8¼"
Leg Length:			
	10"	11"	12¼"

19(21,24) sts rem.

Shoulder Shaping:
Bind off 6(7,8) sts at beg of next row and every other row once.
Work even for 1 row.
Bind off.
Slip next 32(36,38) sts on a stitch holder for back neck.
Join yarn to rem sts and work in pat to end of row. Work to correspond with other side of neck.

FRONT
Work as for Back to **.
Work 1(3,9) rows in pat.

Neck Shaping:
Keeping in pat, work as follows:

Next Row: Work in pat across 28(31,35), turn.

*** Dec one st at neck edge in every row until 19(21,24) sts rem.
Work even for 4(5,6) rows. ***

Shoulder Shaping:
Complete as for Back Shoulder Shaping. Slip next 20(22,22) sts on a stitch holder for front neck.
Join yarn to rem sts and work in pat to end of row.
Rep from *** to ***.
Work even for 9 rows.
Shape shoulder and complete as for other shoulder.

LEFT SLEEVE
Using No. 1 needles and C, cast on 41(45,49) sts.
Work in rib as for lower band of Back, until band measures 3/4" from beg, ending with Row 2 and inc 11 sts evenly across last row — 52(56,60) sts.
Change to No. 3 needles.

☑ A   ☑ C (embroidered on afterwards)
⊟ C (embroidered using stem stitch)

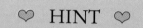

inc one st at each end of 5th and foll 6th(6th,8th) row until there are 60(60,74) sts, then in foll 8th(8th,10th) row until there are 64(70,76) sts.
Work even until length measures 6(7,8¼)", ending with a purl row.

Cap Shaping:
Bind off 8(9,10) sts at beg of next 6 rows.
Bind off rem sts.

RIGHT SLEEVE
Work as for Left Sleeve, using A in place of Mc after needle change.

NECKBAND
Sew right shoulder seam. With right side facing, using No. 1 needles and C, beg at left shoulder and pick up and k 103(113,119) sts, evenly around neck edge (including sts from st holders).
Work in rib as for lower band of Back, beg with Row 2, until neckband measures ¾" from beg, ending with Row 2.
Bind off loosely in rib.

LEFT FRONT SHOULDER BAND
With right side facing, using No. 1 needles and C, pick up and k 19(21,23) sts evenly along left front shoulder edge.
Work 3 rows in rib as for lower band of Back, beg with Row 2.
Next Row: Rib 2(3,4), (bind off 2 sts, rib 4) twice, bind off 2 sts, rib 3(4,5).
Next Row: Rib 3(4,5), (cast on 2 sts, rib 4) twice, cast on 2 sts, rib 2(3,4) — *3 buttonholes made.*
Work 4 rows in rib.
Bind off.

LEFT BACK SHOULDER BAND
Work as for Left Front Shoulder Band omitting buttonholes.

FINISHING
Overlap Front Shoulder Band over Back Shoulder Band, and slipstitch in place at armhole edge. Sew in sleeves, placing center of sleeves at shoulder seams. Sew side and sleeve seams. Sew on buttons.

PANTS
RIGHT LEG
Beg at waist, using No. 1 needles and Mc, cast on 87(91,95) sts.
Row 1: K 2, * p 1, k 1; rep from * to last st, k 1.
Row 2: K 1, * p 1, k 1; rep from * to end.
Rep Rows 1 and 2, 4 times, inc one st in center of last row — 88(92,96) sts.
Change to No. 3 needles.
Work 2 rows in st st.

Back Shaping
Note: To avoid a hole in work, when turning, bring yarn to front of work, slip next stitch onto right-hand needle, with

yarn in back of work, slip the stitch back onto left-hand needle, then turn and proceed as instructed. ****
Row 1: K 12(14,16), turn.
Row 2 and All Even Numbered Rows: Purl.
Row 3: K 19(21,23), turn.
Row 5: K 26(28,30), turn.
Row 7: K 33(35,37), turn.
Continue turning in this manner, working 7 more sts every other row until the Row "k 75(77,79), turn" has been worked.
Next Row: Purl across all sts.
***** Continue in st st, inc one st at each end of Row 9, then every 12th(14th,16th) row until there are 94(98,102) sts.
Work until shorter edge measures 6¼ (6½,7¼)" from beg, ending with a purl row. Mark end of last row.

Leg Shaping:
Dec 1 st at each end of next row and every other row until 68(70,72) sts rem.
Work even for 28(34,40) rows.
Next Row: P 3(4,5), * p 2 tog; rep from * to last 3(4,5) sts, p 3(4,5) — 37(39,41) sts.
Using C, work as follows:
Next Row: Knit.
Work 7 rows in rib as for waist, beg with Row 2.
Bind off loosely in rib.

LEFT LEG
Beg at waist, work as for Right Leg to ****.
Row 1 and All Odd Numbered Rows: Knit.

Row 2: P 12(14,16), turn.
Row 4: P 19(21,23), turn.
Row 6: P 26(28,30), turn.
Row 8: P 33(35,37), turn.
Continue turning in this manner, working 7 sts more every other row until the Row "p 75(77,79), turn" has been worked.
Work as for Right Leg from ***** to end.

FINISHING
Sew Back, Front and Leg seams. Thread elastic through 1st, 5th and 9th rows of rib at waist.

♡ HINT ♡

Baby's knitwear needs to be laundered so often that it's important to wash with care. As a rule of thumb, it is best to follow the washing instructions printed on the label of your yarn. If this is not possible, it is best to wash delicate knits by hand in lukewarm water using mild soap or a soap powder specially formulated for knits.

KNIT A PICTURE

You can work an artist's magic with your knitting needles and a few balls of colored yarn. Stripes are the simplest of all color patterns but it is much easier than you think to knit an entire picture.

Following a graph
Picture patterns are often given in the form of a graph, rather than lengthy written instructions. Each color is represented by a different symbol on the graph. Work the graph from the bottom up, knitting the odd-numbered rows and purling the even-numbered ones. If a pattern is to be repeated, sometimes only one graph is given, with the number of repeats indicated. It is important to keep track of where you are when knitting from a graph so keep a pencil handy to cross out or check rows already worked.

Carrying colors
Colors should be carried across the back of the work for five stitches at most. Ideally, each block of color should be worked from its own ball or bobbin of yarn. This prevents "pulling," and bobbins cut down on the tangle of many balls of yarn. To avoid holes in your knitting, when changing from one color to another, twist the new color around the color just used.

LEMON CROCHET JACKET AND BONNET

TECHNIQUE: Crocheting

DIRECTIONS
JACKET
Beg at neck, using hook ch 62.

Row 1: Skip 1 ch, sc in each ch to end —
61sc.

Row 2 (right side): (Sc, ch 1) in first sc, *
ch 1, sk next 2 sc, "cluster" in next st, ch 1,
sk next 2 sc, dc in next sc; rep from * to end
— 10 "clusters."

Row 3: (Sc, ch 1) in first dc, dc in ch-1 sp,
ch 1, "cluster" in ch-1 sp of cluster from
previous row, * ch 1, dc in next ch-1 sp, dc
in next dc, dc in next ch-1 sp, ch-1, cluster
in ch-1 sp of cluster from previous row; rep
from * but end with ch 1, dc in next ch-1 sp,
dc in top of turning-ch.

Row 4: (Sc, ch 1) in first dc, dc in next dc,
dc in next ch-1 sp, * ch 1, cluster in ch-1 sp
of cluster from previous row, ch 1, dc in
next ch-sp, dc in each of next 3 dc, dc in
next ch-sp; rep from * until 1 cluster remains, ch 1, cluster in ch-1 sp of cluster
from previous row, ch 1, dc in next ch-sp,
dc in next dc, dc in top of turning-ch.

Row 5: (Sc, ch 1) in first dc, dc in each of
next 2 dc, dc in next ch-sp, * ch 1, cluster
in ch-1 sp of cluster from previous row, ch
1, dc in next ch-1 sp, dc in each of next 5
dc, dc in next ch-1 sp; rep from * until 1
cluster remains, ch 1, cluster in ch-1 sp of
cluster from previous row, ch 1, dc in next
ch-1 sp, dc in each of next 2 dc, dc in top
of turning-ch.

Rows 6-8: Rep Row 5, 3 times more,
working 2 dc more between clusters and 1
dc more at each end of each row. (There
should be 13 dc between each cluster and
7 dc at each end upon completion of Row
8.)

Row 9: (Sc, ch 1) in first dc, dc in each of
next 6 dc, * ch 1, cluster in ch-1 sp of
cluster from previous row, ch 1, dc in each
of next 13 dc; rep from * until 1 cluster
remains, ch 1, cluster in ch-1 sp of cluster
from previous row, ch 1, dc in each of next
6 dc, dc in top of turning-ch.

SIZE
Directions are given for size 6 months.

MATERIALS
Sport-Weight Yarn (50 gr. ball): 3 balls
for Jacket and 1 ball for Bonnet; Size C
crochet hook, *or any size hook to obtain
gauge below*; tapestry needle.

GAUGE
23 dc = 4"; 12 rows = 4"; 4 clusters = 4";
20 rows = 4". Be sure to check your
gauge.

MEASUREMENTS
Size:	6 mos.
Body Chest:	18"
Finished Measurements:	
Chest:	18"
Length:	9 1/2"
Sleeve Length:	5"
Bonnet fits around face:	10"

STITCHES
Cluster: (3dc, ch 1, 3dc) all in same st.

Row 10: (Sc, ch 1) in first dc, sk dc, cluster
in next dc, sk dc, dc in next dc, sk dc,
cluster in next dc, dc in first dc of cluster,
cluster in ch-1 sp of cluster from previous
row, dc in last dc of cluster, (cluster in next
dc, sk 2 dc, dc in next dc, sk 2 dc) twice,
cluster in next dc, dc in first dc of cluster,
3 dc in ch-1 sp of cluster from previous
row, ch 1, sk last 3 dc of cluster, (dc in each
of next 13 dc, cluster in ch-1 sp of cluster
from previous row, sk last 3 dc of cluster,
dc in each of next 13 dc) for first Sleeve, ch
1, 3 dc in ch-1 sp in center of next cluster,
dc in last dc of same cluster, (cluster in
next dc, sk 2 dc, dc in next dc, sk 2 dc)
twice, cluster in next dc, dc in first dc of
next cluster, cluster in ch-1 sp of cluster
from previous row, dc in last dc of cluster,
(cluster in next dc, sk 2 dc, dc in next dc,
sk 2 dc) twice, cluster in next dc, dc in first
dc of next cluster, cluster in ch-1 sp of
cluster from previous row, dc in last dc of
cluster, (cluster in next dc, sk 2 dc, dc in
next dc, sk 2 dc) twice, cluster in next dc,
dc in first dc of next cluster, 3 dc in ch-1 sp
of cluster from previous row, ch 1, sk last
3 dc of cluster, (dc in each of next 13 dc,
cluster in ch-1 sp of cluster from previous
row, dc in each of next 13 dc) for 2nd
Sleeve, ch 1, 3 dc in ch-1 sp of next cluster,
dc in last dc of same cluster, (cluster in
next dc, sk 2 dc, dc in next dc, sk 2 dc)
twice, cluster in next dc, dc in first dc of

next cluster, cluster in ch-1 sp of cluster from previous row, dc in last dc of same cluster, cluster in next dc, sk dc, dc in next dc, sk 1 dc, cluster in next dc, sk dc, dc in top of turning-ch.

Row 11: (Sc, ch 1) in first dc, (cluster in ch-1 sp of cluster from previous row, dc in next dc) 6 times, 3 dc in next ch-1 sp, sk next (13 dc, cluster, 13 dc), ch 1, 3 dc in next ch-1 sp, sk 3 dc, (dc in next dc, cluster in ch-1 sp of cluster from previous row) 11 times, dc in next dc, 3 dc in next ch-1 sp, ch 1, sk next (13 dc, cluster, 13 dc), ch 1, 3 dc in next ch 1 sp, sk 3 dc, (dc in next dc, cluster in ch-1 sp of cluster from previous row) 6 times, dc in top of turning-ch.

Continue on this section for Back and Fronts as follows:

Row 12: (Sc, ch 1) in first dc, (cluster in ch-1 sp of cluster from previous row, dc in next dc) 6 times, sk 3 dc, cluster in next ch-1 sp, sk 3 dc, (dc in next dc, cluster in next ch-1 sp of cluster from previous row) 11 times, dc in next dc, sk 3 dc, cluster in next ch-1 sp, sk 3 dc, (dc in next dc, cluster in next ch-1 sp of cluster from previous row) 6 times, dc in top of turning-ch.

Row 13: (Sc, ch 1) in first dc, * cluster in next ch-1 sp of cluster from previous row, dc in next dc; rep from * to end, working last dc in top of turning-ch.

Rep Row 13, 11 times more.

Do not fasten off.

Continue up right front edge as follows:

Next Row: Ch 2, sc in first dc, 2 sc in each dc to neck edge, sc in side of 1st row, 2 sc in corner, sc in each of next 61sc of foundation row, 2 sc in corner, sc in side of 1st row, 2 sc in each dc to lower edge. Fasten off.

Neck Edging:
With right side of work facing, join yarn to right neck edge inside 2 corner sc, (sc, ch 1) in next sc, * sk 2 sc, cluster in next sc, sk 2 sc, dc in next sc; rep from * to other corner. Fasten off.

SLEEVES
With wrong side facing, join yarn with a sl st in ch-1 sp at underarm.

Row 1: (Sc, ch 1) in ch 1-sp, (cluster in next dc, sk 2 dc, dc in next dc, sk 2 dc) twice, cluster in next dc, dc in first dc of cluster, cluster in ch-1 sp of cluster from previous row, dc in last dc of cluster, (cluster in next dc, sk 2 dc, dc in next dc, sk 2 dc) twice, cluster in next dc, dc in ch-1 sp at underarm, turn.

Row 2: (Sc, ch 1) in first dc, * cluster in ch-1 sp of cluster from previous row, dc in

next dc; rep from * to end, working last dc in top of turning-ch, then join with a sl st to beg of row.

Note: Work sleeve in rounds from this point on.

Rnd 1: Ch 3, * cluster in ch-1 sp of cluster from previous row, dc in next dc; rep from * to last cluster, cluster in ch-1 sp of cluster from previous row, sl st in ch-3 at beg.

Rnd 2: Ch 3, (dc, ch 1, dc) in ch-1 sp of cluster from previous round, dc in next dc, * cluster in ch-1 sp of cluster from previous round, dc in next dc; rep from * to last cluster, (dc, ch 1, dc) in ch-1 sp of cluster from previous round, sl st in ch-3 at beg.

Rnd 3: Ch 3, (dc, ch 1, dc) in next ch-1 sp, dc in next dc; rep from * of Rnd 2 to last ch-1 sp, (dc, ch 1, dc) in last ch-1 sp, sl st in ch-3 at beg.

Rep Rnd 3 twice.

Rnd 6: Ch 3, 2 dc in same place as sl st, sk (dc, ch 1, dc), dc in next dc, * cluster in ch-1 sp of cluster from previous round, dc in next dc; rep from * 4 times more, sk (dc, ch 1, dc), 3 dc between last dc and next dc, ch 1, sl st in ch-3 at beg.

Rnd 7: Ch 3, cluster back into last ch-1 sp between beg and end of Rnd 6, dc in next dc, * cluster in ch-1 sp of cluster from previous round, dc in next dc; rep from * to end, sl st in ch-3 at beg.

Rnd 8: Ch 3, cluster in ch-1 sp of cluster from previous round, dc in next dc; rep from * to last cluster, cluster in ch-1 sp of

last cluster, sl st in ch-3 at beg. Rep Rnd 8, 3 times. Fasten off.

FINISHING
Sew underarm seams. Using 3 strands of yarn (each 100" long), make a twisted cord and thread through double crochets between clusters at neck edge for ties.

BONNET
Using hook ch 13.
Row 1: Sc in 2nd ch from hook, sc in each ch to end.
Row 2: (Sc, ch 1, dc) in first sc, 2 dc in each of next 10 sc, 2 dc in top of turning-ch — 24 sts.
Row 3: (Sc, ch 1) in first dc, 2 dc in next dc, * dc in next dc, 2 dc in next dc; rep from * to last 2 sts, dc in next dc, dc in top of turning-ch — 35 sts.
Row 4: (Sc, ch 1) in first dc, dc in next dc, 2 dc in next dc, * dc in each of next 2 dc, 2 dc in next dc; rep from * to last 2 sts, dc in next dc, dc in top of turning-ch — 46 sts.
Row 5: (Sc, ch 1) in first dc, dc in next dc, 2 dc in next dc, * dc in each of next 3 dc, 2 dc in next dc; rep from * to last 3 sts, dc in each of next 2 dc, dc in top of turning-ch — 57 sts.
Row 6: (Sc, ch 1) in first dc, dc in each of next 3 dc, 2 dc in next dc, * dc in each of next 15 dc, 2 dc in next dc; rep from * to last 4 sts, dc in each of next 3 dc, dc in top of turning-ch — 61 sts.

Beg pattern as follows:
Row 1: (Sc, ch 1) in first dc, * sk next 2 dc, cluster in next dc, sk next 2 dc, dc in next dc; rep from * to end, working last dc in top of turning-ch — 9 clusters.
Row 2: (Sc, ch 1) in first dc, * cluster in ch-1 sp of cluster from previous row, dc in next dc; rep from * to end, working last dc in top of turning-ch.
Rep Row 2 10 times.
Do not fasten off.
Thread a length of yarn through the stitches of foundation chain row, pull up tightly and fasten off securely. Sew back seam for 2" from foundation row.
Work 1 row of sc evenly along side edges of Bonnet (excluding last row of pat). Fasten off.

FINISHING
Using 3 strands of yarn (each 118" long), make a twisted cord and thread through last row of pat for ties.

BABY BUNNY

TECHNIQUE: Sewing

MATERIALS
☐ scrap of cotton fabric
☐ polyester fiberfill for stuffing
☐ 8 inches of ½"-wide ribbon
☐ embroidery floss
☐ tracing paper

DIRECTIONS
1 Trace full-size pattern *(see this page)* onto tracing paper.
2 From fabric, cut out two bunny shapes, ³/₈" seam allowed. Embroider face on bunny, using satin stitch for eyes and nose, and stem stitch for mouth.
3 Sew front and back together, with right sides facing and leaving a small opening for turning below arm. Reinforce corners with second row of stitching. Clip seams, turn and press.
4 Stuff lightly with fiberfill. Slipstitch opening closed. Tie bow around neck.

Sunshine

Let the sun shine in with these delicious baby things. Combine traditional styles with these happy colors, decked out in polka dots, stripes and even ducks. There are frills and flounces for the baby girl and a cute knitted set, perfect for every baby.

DUCKLING OUTFIT

TECHNIQUE: Knitting

DIRECTIONS
CARDIGAN
BACK
Using No. 3 needles and Mc, cast on 53(61,67) sts.

Row 1: K 2, *p 1, k 1; rep from * to last st, k 1.

Row 2: K 1, *p 1, k 1; rep from * to end.
Rep Rows 1 and 2 until lower band measures 1¼" from beg, ending with Row 2, inc 7 sts evenly across last row — 60(68,74) sts.

Change to No. 5 needles and A.

Work 4 rows in st st (k 1 row , p 1 row).

Continue in st st, working in stripes of 2 rows B, 2 rows A, 2 rows Mc and 2 rows A, until work measures 8½(9½,10½)" from beg, ending with a purl row.

Shoulder Shaping:
Bind off 7(8,9) sts at beg of next 4 rows, then 7(8,8) sts at beg of next 2 rows.
Slip rem 18(20,22) sts on a stitch holder for back neck.

LEFT FRONT
Using No. 3 needles and Mc, cast on 27(31,33) sts.

Work in rib as for lower band of Back, until band measures 1¼" from beg, ending with Row 2, inc 3(3,4) sts evenly across last row — 30(34,37) sts.

Change to No. 5 needles and A.
Work 4 rows in st st.

Continue in st st working in stripes as for Back until there are 34(36,40) rows less than back to shoulder shaping.

Front Neck Shaping:
Continue in stripes as established, dec one st at end (neck edge) of next, then every 4th (2nd, 2nd) row 8(2,2) times more, **2nd and 3rd sizes only**: then every 4th row 7(8) times — 21(24,26) sts.
Work even for 1(3,3) rows.

Shoulder Shaping:
Bind off 7(8,9) sts at beg of next, then every other row once.
Work even for 1 row. Bind off rem sts.

RIGHT FRONT
Work to correspond with Left Front.

SLEEVES
Using No. 3 needles and Mc, cast on

SIZE
Directions are given for size 3 months. Changes for 6 months and 9 months are in parentheses.

MATERIALS
Sport-Weight Yarn (50 gr. ball): 1(1,2) balls of main color (Mc), 1(1,2) balls of white (A) , 1 ball of yellow (B) for Cardigan; 1(1, 2) balls of Mc, 2(2, 3) balls of A, 1 ball of B, small amount each of red (C) and black (D) for Pullover; 2(3, 3) balls of Mc, 1 ball each of A and B, a small amt. of C and D for Overalls; 1 ball each of Mc and A for Booties; 1 pair each No. 3 and No. 5 knitting needles, *or any size needles to obtain gauge below*; 1 stitch holder and 4 buttons for Cardigan; bobbins; 2 stitch holders and 6 buttons for Pullover; 2 buttons, bobbins and elastic for Overalls; 1 yard of ¼"-wide ribbons for Booties; tapestry needle.

GAUGE
On No. 5 needles in stockinette stitch (st st) — 13 sts = 2"; 9 rows = 1". Be sure to check your gauge.

MEASUREMENTS

Sizes (mos.):	3	6	9
Body Chest:	16"	18"	20"
Finished Measurements:			
Cardigan Chest:	19"	21"	23"
Length to back neck:			
	8½"	9½"	10½"
Sleeve Length:	5"	6"	7"
Pullover Chest:	18"	20"	22"
Length to Back Neck:			
	8½"	9½"	10½"
Sleeve Length:	5"	6"	7"
Overall Outer Leg Length:			
		13"	15"	17"
Booties - Length of Foot:			3½"

(Fits approximately 3 mos. - 7 mos.)

35(35,37) sts.
Work in rib as for lower band of Back until band measures 1¼" from beg, ending with Row 2 and inc 4 sts evenly across last row — 39(39,41) sts.
Change to No. 5 needles and A.
Work 2 rows in st st.

Continue in stripes of 2 rows A, 2 rows B, 2 rows A and 2 rows Mc throughout. **At the same time,** inc one st at each end of next row, then every 6th(4th,4th) row 4(3,5) more times, **2nd and 3rd sizes only:** Then every 6th row 3 times — 49(53,59) sts.

Continue in stripes until length measures 5(6,7)" from beg, working last row on wrong side.

Cap Shaping:
Bind off 7(8,9) sts at beg of next 4 rows, then 7(7,8) sts at beg of next 2 rows.
Bind off.

FRONT BAND
Sew shoulder seams. With right side facing, using No. 3 needles and Mc, pick up and k 38(44,50) sts evenly along lower Right Front edge to beg of front neck shaping, pick up and k 34(36,40) sts evenly along right front neck edge, k across 18(20,22) sts from back neck stitch holder, inc one st in center, pick up and k 34(36,40) sts evenly along left front neck edge to where shaping begins, and pick up and k 38(44,50) sts evenly along lower Left Front edge — 163(181,203) sts.

Work 1 row in rib as for lower band of Back.

Next row: Rib 4,[k 2 tog, yo, rib 8(10,12)] 3 times, k 2 tog, yo, rib to end — *4 buttonholes made.*
Work 3 rows in rib.
Bind off loosely in rib.

FINISHING
Sew in sleeves, placing center of sleeves at shoulder seams. Sew side and sleeve seams. Sew on buttons.

PULLOVER
BACK
Using No. 3 needles and Mc, cast on 53(61,67) sts.

Row 1: K 2, *p 1, k 1; rep from * to last st, k 1.

Row 2: K 1, *p 1, k 1; rep from * to end.
Rep Rows 1 and 2 until lower band measures 1¼" from beg, ending with Row 2 and inc 7 sts evenly across last row — 60(68,74) sts.

Change to No. 5 needles.
Work 2 rows st st (k 1 row , p 1 row).

Note: When working Duck Motif (chart A) carry colors not in use loosely across wrong side of work. Always carry colors to end of rows. When following chart A, work k rows from right to left and p rows from left to right.

Note: When changing colors, pick up new color from under the color being used, twisting yarns on wrong side of work to prevent holes. Use a separate bobbin for each color change.

Row 3: * K 2 A, k 2 Mc; rep from * to last 0(0,2) sts, k 0(0,2) A.

Row 4: P 17(21,24) A, p 5 B, p 15 A, p 5 B, p 18(22,25) A.

Work Rows 5 to 22 following chart A.

Row 23: *K 2 Mc, k 2 A; rep from * to last 0(0,2) sts, k 0(0,2) Mc.

Using A, continue in st st until work measures 8½(9½,10½)" from beg, ending with a purl row.

Mark each end of last row.

Shoulder Shaping:

Next row: K 21(24,26), turn.

** Bind off 2 sts at beg of next and every other row until 3(2,4) sts rem.

Bind off **.

Slip next 18(20,22) sts onto a stitch holder for back neck.

Join yarn to rem sts and k to end.

Work even for 1 row.

Rep from ** to **.

FRONT

Work as for Back until there are 14(14,16) rows less than back to shoulder shaping.

Neck Shaping:

Next row: K 25(28,31), turn.

Dec one st at neck edge every other row 4(4,5) times — 21(24,26) sts.

Work even for 6 rows.

Mark each end of last row.

Shoulder Shaping:

Complete as for back shoulder from ** to **

Slip next 10(12,12) sts onto a stitch holder for front neck.

Join yarn to rem sts and work to corre-

spond with other side, reversing shaping.

SLEEVES

Using No. 3 needles and Mc, cast on 33(37,39) sts.

Work in rib as for lower band of Back until band measures 1¼" from beg, working last row on wrong side and inc 4 sts evenly across last row — 37(41,43) sts.

Change to No. 5 needles and A.

Continue in st st, working stripes of 2 rows

A and 2 rows Mc throughout, **at the same time** inc one st at each end of 3rd, then 6th(6th,8th) rows until there are 47(47,55) sts.

2nd size only: then in foll 8th row twice — 47(51, 55) sts.

Continue in stripes without shaping until length measures 5(6,7)" from beg, ending with a purl row.

Cap Shaping:

GRAPH A

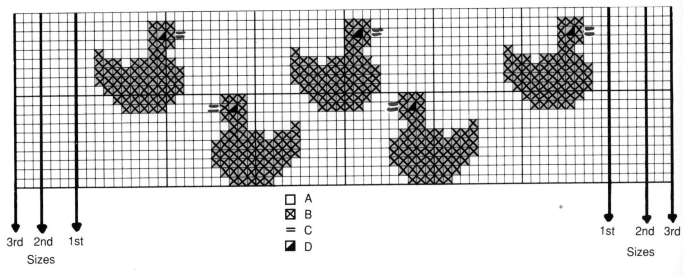

	A
☒	B
=	C
◪	D

3rd 2nd 1st

Sizes

1st 2nd 3rd

Sizes

Bind off 7(7,8) sts at beg of next 4 rows, then 6(8,8) sts at beg of next 2 rows. Bind off rem sts.

BACK NECKBAND

Using No. 3 needles and Mc, with right side facing, pick up and k 34(36,38) sts evenly along right back shoulder edge, k across 18(20,22) sts from back neck stitch holder, dec one st in center, and pick up and k 34(36,38) sts evenly along left back shoulder edge — 85(91,97) sts.

Next row: Using Mc, purl.

Work 2 rows rib, as for lower band of Back.

Next row: Rib 4(4,5), [yo, k 2 tog, rib 8(9,10)] twice, yo, k 2 tog, rib 33(35,35), [yo, k 2 tog, rib 8(9,10)] twice, yo, k 2 tog, rib 4(4,5) — 6 buttonholes made.

Work 3 rows rib, beg with Row 2. Bind off loosely in rib.

FRONT NECKBAND

Using No. 3 needles and A, with right side facing, pick up and k 42(44,46) sts evenly along front left shoulder and side neck edge, k across 10(12,12) sts from front stitch holder, inc one st in center and pick up and k 42(44,46) sts evenly along right shoulder and side neck edge — 95(101,105) sts.

Next row: Using Mc, purl.

Work 6 rows rib as for lower band of Back. Bind off loosely in rib.

FINISHING

With wrong sides of Front and Back together, overlap shoulders, matching markers, and tack shoulder seams together at side edges. Sew in sleeves, placing center of sleeve at shoulder seams. Sew side and sleeve seams. Sew on buttons. Embroider beaks in C as shown. Using duplicate stitch and D, embroider eyes on ducks.

OVERALLS

RIGHT LEG

Beg at waist, using No. 3 needles and Mc, cast on 57(63,69) sts.

Row 1: K 2, *p 1, k 1; rep from * to last st, k 1.

Row 2: K 1, *p 1, k 1; rep from * to end. Rep Rows 1 and 2 once.

Buttonhole row: Rib 20, yo, k 2 tog, rib to end.

Rep Row 2, then Row 1 once, then Row 2 once.

Change to No. 5 needles.

Work 2 rows in st st.

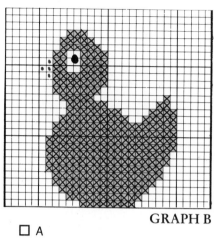

□ A

☒ B

⊡ C (embroidered on afterwards)

GRAPH B

Note: To avoid holes in work, when turning, bring yarn to front of work, slip next st onto right-hand needle, with yarn in back of work, slip st back onto left-hand needle, then turn and proceed as instructed. ***.

Row 1: K 16, turn.

Row 2 and All Even Numbered Rows: Purl.

Row 3: K 22, turn.

Row 5: K 28, turn.

Continue turning in this manner, working 6 more sts in every knit row until the Row "k 46(52,58) turn" has been worked.

Next row: Rep Row 2.

Continue in st st, inc one st at each end of 7th, then every 6th row until there are 69(75,81) sts.

Continue until short side measures 6¼ (6½,7)" from beg, ending with a purl row.

Crotch Shaping:

Bind off 3 sts at beg of next 2 rows.

Dec one st at each end of next, then every other row 5 times more — 51(57,63) sts.

Continue in st st (beg with a purl row) without shaping until work measures 12(14,16)" from beg, ending with a purl row.

Change to No. 3 needles.

Work 1 row in rib as for waistband, dec 6(6,8) sts evenly across — 45(51,55) sts.

Continue in rib for 1¼", beg and ending with Row 2.

Bind off loosely in rib.

LEFT LEG

Work to correspond with Right Leg to ***, working buttonhole row as follows: Rib to last 22 sts, k 2 tog, yo, rib 20.

Row 1 and All Odd Numbered Rows: Knit.

Row 2: P 16, turn.

Row 4: P 22, turn.

Continue turning in this manner, working 6 more sts in every purl row until the row "p 46(52,58), turn" has been worked.

Work to correspond with Left Front reversing shaping.

FRONT BIB

Sew front, back and leg seams.

Place a marker 3¼" from either side of center front seam.

Using No. 5 needles and Mc, pick up and k 42 sts evenly between markers.

Row 1: K 6 Mc, p 30 A, k 6 Mc.

Row 2: K 6 Mc, k 30 A, k 6 Mc.

Next row: Rep Row 1.

Next row: K 6 Mc, work Row 1 of chart B across next 30 sts, k 6 Mc.

Next row: K 6 Mc, work Row 2 of chart B across next 30 sts, k 6 Mc.

Work chart B as established until completion of Row 28.

Next row: Knit.

Rep last row 5 times.

Next row: K 6, bind off 30 sts, k 6.

RIGHT SHOULDER STRAP

Continue in garter st (k every row) on last 6 sts until strap measures 8½(9½,10)" from beg. Bind off.

LEFT SHOULDER STRAP

Join yarn to rem 6 sts and work to correspond with Right Shoulder Strap.

FINISHING

Sew buttons to end of straps. Thread elastic through first, last and center row of rib at waist. Using duplicate stitch and C, embroider beak. Using D, embroider eye as shown.

BOOTIES

Begin at center of sole, using No. 5 needles and Mc, cast on 35 sts.
Row 1: Knit.
Row 2: Purl.
Row 3: K 1, inc in next st, k 14, inc in next st, k 1, inc in next st, k 14, inc in next st, k 1 — 39 sts.
Row 4: Purl.
Row 5: K 1, inc in next st, k 16, inc in next st, k 1, inc in next st, k 16, inc in next st, k 1 — 43 sts.
Row 6: Purl.
Row 7: K 1, inc in next st, k 18, inc in next st, k 1, inc in next st, k 18, inc in next st, k 1 — 47 sts.
Row 8: Purl.
Row 9: K 1, inc in next st, k 20, inc in next st, k 1, inc in next st, k 20, inc in next st, k 1 — 51 sts.
Row 10: Knit.
Work 6 rows in st st (k 1 row, p 1 row), in stripes of 2 rows Mc, 2 rows A and 2 rows Mc.

Instep shaping:
Using Mc, work as follows:
Row 1: K 30, k 2 tog, turn.
Row 2: P 10, p 2 tog, turn.
Row 3: K10, k 2 tog, turn.
Row 4: Rep Row 2.
Rep Rows 3 and 4, 6 times.
Row 17: Knit to end.
Row 18: Purl across all 35 sts.
Row 19: K 1, *yo, k 2 tog; rep from * to end.
Row 20: Purl.
Change to No. 3 needles and A.

Row 21: Knit.
Row 22: K 1, *p 1, k 1; rep from * to end.
Using B; rep Rows 21 and 22 once.
Using A; rep Rows 21 and 22 once.
Row 27: Using A, k 2, *p 1, k 1; rep from * to last st, k 1.
Rep Rows 22 and 27, 3 times.
Bind off loosely in rib.

FINISHING

Press lightly with a damp cloth and a cool iron. Sew foot, heel and back seams. Thread ribbon through eyelet holes of Row 19 and tie in a bow at center front.

CHECK YOUR GAUGE

Correct gauge is essential for perfect fit and shape in knitted and crocheted work.

What is gauge?
Gauge, or tension, is simply a way of measuring the tightness or looseness of your stitching. It is affected by the type and thickness of your yarn, needle or hook size and whether the work is plain, or patterned.

If your tension is too loose (too few stitches per inch), your garment will lack shape, stretch easily and wash poorly. If your tension is too tight (too many stitches per inch), your piece will feel stiff and will not be comfortable to wear.

How to measure gauge?
Every knitting and crochet pattern in this book specifies a gauge, usually stitches-per-inch.
To measure your gauge, knit or crochet a 5- or 6-inch test square in your stitch pattern. End off, then press your sample lightly, if necessary. Pin your square on a firm surface. Align the top of a ruler with a row of stitches. Place a pin at 0, and another at 4 inches. Count the stitches between the pins. To measure row gauge, place the ruler vertically.

Adjusting your gauge
If you have too few stitches per inch, use finer needles or a smaller hook. If you have too many stitches per inch, use thicker needles or a larger hook. If you use a heavier yarn than the one specified in the pattern, you will count fewer stitches per inch. A finer yarn will yield more stitches per inch. Remember if you change yarn, needles, hooks or pattern, you must knit a new gauge square and adjust your needles or hook accordingly.

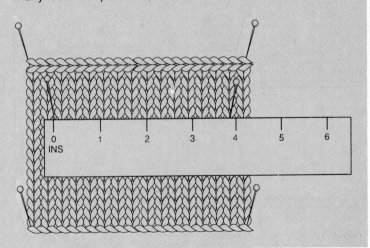

YELLOW DOTTED DRESS

(See photograph of dress on page 17)

TECHNIQUE: Sewing

SIZE: 6 to 12 months

MATERIALS
- [ ] 1⅞ yards of 45"-wide voile
- [ ] 3 buttons about ⅜" dia.
- [ ] 4 yards ½"-wide single-fold bias tape
- [ ] elastic - 1½ yards ⅛"-wide and ¾ yard ¼"-wide
- [ ] tracing paper
- [ ] sewing thread to match fabric

NOTE: The yoke is faced and there is a center back opening that extends into the skirt. To "cut a pair," pin the pattern to folded fabric. Seam ⅜" deep with the pieces pinned right sides together.

DIRECTIONS
Pattern outline 〰〰〰〰〰〰

1 Pattern: Trace the full-size patterns, Nos. 13 through 18 (see the pullout sheet and pattern outline above).

2 Cutting: With center front on the fold of doubled fabric, cut two #13 front yokes (one will be a facing) and one # 14 front skirt. With the center back on the fold of doubled fabric, cut two #15 back yokes. (Each back yoke will fold in half at the back opening to make its own facing.) Cut 1 pair each of #17 sleeves, #16 back skirts and #18 panties. **For ruffles,** cut 3"-wide strips of fabric and piece them to make ¾ yard for neck edge, 2 yards for the other yoke edges and 3 yards for the hem edge.

3 Yoke: Seam each yoke back to a yoke front at the shoulder edges. (The yoke backs will overlap each other for the time being.) Unfold the bias tape so its raw edges match and stitch it, along its original folds, to the armholes and bottom edges of the yoke with right sides together, raw edges outward and the stitching ⅜" from the yoke edges.

4 Yoke Ruffle: Fold the 2-yard ruffle strip in half with right sides together and seam both short ends. Turn it right side out and press. Stitch a gathering row ¼" from the raw edges. With right sides together and raw edges even, pin each end of the ruffle to the center back line (see pattern) of a back yoke *without pinning through the extending facing*. Pin the ruffle center at the CF bottom of the yoke. Halfway between, pin the ruffle to a shoulder seam. Pull up thread and make gathers to fit the front yoke; stitch.

5 Back Skirt: From the hem edge upward, seam the back skirts up the center, stopping ¼" above the right angle that turns outward to make a facing. Turn under ¼" at the facing's long edge and stitch.

6 Assembly: Gather top edge of front skirt between notches (see pattern). Gather back skirt from a notch to the CB line (see pattern). Pin yoke to skirts with CF's matching, side edges even and the CB's (see pattern) lined up. Pull up gathers to fit yoke; stitch.

7 Yoke Facing: With right sides together, fold each back yoke in half. Pin its shoulder edge to one of the front yoke facing: stitch and press seams open. Turn the yoke right side out (along with the skirt edge) and press the folded back edges. Baste raw edges together at neck and armholes. Turn under the yoke facing's bottom edge and slipstitch it to the yoke seam.

8 Neck Edge: Prepare a 27" ruffle, as you did the yoke ruffle and stitch it to the neck edge. Then bind the neck edge with bias tape, turning under both raw ends.

9 Sleeves: Gather top edge of each sleeve between notches. Pin sleeves to dress at yoke and armhole edges. Draw up gathers to fit; stitch. Press ruffle downward toward sleeves and skirt. Topstitch around the yoke near the piping. At the wrist edge, turn under 1¾" and press. Turn under the raw edge and stitch the 1½" hem. Stitch again ¼" away to make a casing. Insert 6"-long ⅛" elastic and stitch across each end.

10 Underarm/Side Seam: Seam front to back at sleeve and side edges, matching armholes, casing and finished edge.

11 Lower Edge: Apply bias tape to the lower edge as you did in Step 3. Seam the short ends of a 3-yard ruffle strip and press the seam open. Fold this loop in half and press. Gather the raw edges and apply the ruffle over the piping as on the yoke. Press the seam upward and topstitch near the piping through all layers.

12 Back Opening: Make buttonholes and sew on buttons.

13 Panties: Seam the pair of pantie pieces at the CB and CF edges (they are the 2 curved ones that start at the top, straight edge). Press the seams open. With the two center seams matching, seam the crotch - the 2 shortest edges. Finish leg edges with a narrow hem. About ⅜" above the hem on the inside, zigzag across ⅛" elastic, stretching it slightly as you sew, and fasten both ends. Stitch a hem ½" wide at the waist and insert a 20" piece of ¼" elastic; bring the ends together and stitch them to fit.

♡ HINT ♡

When choosing buttons for the back of a baby's dress, select those that are flat and smooth. Remember that babies spend many hours lying on their backs and shanks and rough surfaces on buttons will make them uncomfortable.

Loose buttons are a very serious hazard for babies, so make sure you sew them on very securely. Always use your thread doubled, or buttonhole thread which is much stronger than ordinary thread. Anchor your first and last stitches well and check buttons regularly to spot a loose one.

Remember there are a number of very suitable alternatives to buttons such as ties and Velcro.

SHEET WITH DOTTED BORDER

TECHNIQUE: Sewing

MATERIALS
- ☐ 1 ³/₄ yards of 45"-wide cream voile
- ☐ ¹/₄ yard of 45"-wide dotted voile
- ☐ 1¹/₄ yard of bias binding

DIRECTIONS
1 Border: Stitch dotted voile to a 45"-edge of the cream voile, with right side of the trim against the wrong side of the sheet. Fold the trim double with wrong sides together. Turn it to the right side of the sheet; press.

2 Binding: Slide the raw edges of the bias binding under the folded edge of the trim and pin it. Stitch along the folded edge through all thicknesses to finish border.

YELLOW STRIPED SLEEP SUIT

TECHNIQUE: Sewing

SIZE: 0 to 6 months

MATERIALS
- ☐ 1¹/₄ yards of 45"-wide fabric
- ☐ 18" zipper
- ☐ ³/₈ yard ¹/₈" elastic
- ☐ tracing paper
- ☐ sewing thread to match fabric

NOTE: To "cut a pair," pin the pattern to folded fabric. Seam ³/₈" deep with the pieces pinned right sides together.

DIRECTIONS
Pattern outline ──────────
1 Pattern: Trace the full-size patterns, Nos. 7 through 12 (see pullout sheet and the pattern outline above) including the

---

BABY'S BEDTIME

Keeping your baby comfortably warm and covered all through the night is simple with a pretty and practical sleep suit. Blankets and sheets are often kicked off, especially as your baby grows more active. Use a fitted sheet to cover the mattress and a one-piece suit, made of a fabric appropriate to the season, which covers baby from top to toe. Choose cotton or stretch terry cloth for those in-between nights and brushed cotton or fine wool for cooler weather. For really chilly nights, add a zippered or buttoned sleeping bag (page 36) for extra warmth.

3 Edges: At the 3 unfinished edges, turn under ¹/₄" , then ³/₈" and stitch.

grainlines, "on fold" edges and CF and CB labels. Also mark the A and B locations on the 2 fronts and the front leg extension.

2 Cutting: Cut 1 each of #7 right front, #8 left front extension and #9 left front. Cut 1 pair each of #10 backs and #12 sleeves.

With its CB on a fold of material cut the #11 collar twice.

3 Leg Extension: With right sides together, stitch the leg extension to the right front. With the A locations matching and crotch edges even, seam the short curved edge, then continue down the shorter of the other two edges to the foot. Pin the 2 fronts together with edges matching and stitch the free edge of the extension to the left front up as far as the B position (where the zipper will begin). Unpin the fronts.

4 Zipper: Turn under ³/₈" at each front edge and press. Apply a zipper beneath the pressed edges with the pull tab ¹/₂" below the neck edge.

5 Back: At the ankle of the back pieces, bring the pair of horizontal lines together, wrong sides facing, and stitch across them to make a pleat. Seam the 2 back pieces at the center back.

6 Bias Piping: Cut six 8"-long x 1"-wide bias strips. Fold them in half, wrong sides facing, and press. Baste a strip to each raglan (slanted) armhole with right sides together and raw edges matching; stitch. In the same way, baste the other 2 strips to the wrist edge of the sleeves. Cut a 28"-long (pieced as needed) x 1" bias strip and stitch it in the same way to the outside edge of one collar.

7 Sleeves: Seam the longer armhole edge of each sleeve to the sleep suit back. Seam the opposite sleeve edges to the suit front.

8 Collar: Seam the second collar piece (the facing) to the piped collar at the outside edges. Clip the seam allowance. Turn it right side out and press. Baste the collar to the neck edge of the suit with right sides up, matching the CB's and the CF's. Cut a 1¹/₂"-wide bias strip about 14" long. Turning under each end, baste the strip over the collar at the neck edge with right sides together and raw edges even. Stitch through all layers. Turn the bias strip toward the inside, turn under its raw edge and slipstitch it to the sleep suit.

9 Wrists: Turn the piping downward and stitch along the raw edges inside the sleeve. Into this "casing" insert 6"-long narrow elastic and stitch across both ends.

10 Assembly: Pin the raw edges of the suit together and sew one continuous seam from wrist to wrist.

First Smiles

A baby's first smile is a special moment to be treasured. Your baby will be picture perfect in these lovely garments of traditional pink, blue and white. There's an outfit for every babe, no matter what time of year, and some sweet touches for the nursery, featuring a bunny or two.

PINK, BLUE AND WHITE BABY'S SHAWL COLLAR CARDIGAN

TECHNIQUE: Knitting

DIRECTIONS
BACK
Using No. 1 needles and Mc, cast on 74(82,90) sts.

Row 1: K 2, * p 2, k 2; rep from * to end.
Row 2: P 2, * k 2, p 2; rep from * to end.
Rep Rows 1 and 2 until lower band measures 1¹/2" from beg, ending with Row 2 and inc 0(2,2) sts evenly across last row — 74(84,92) sts.
Change to No. 3 needles.
Continue in st st (k 1 row, p 1 row) until work measures 5¹/2(6,7)" from beg, ending with a purl row.
Armhole Shaping:
Bind off 4(5,5) sts at beg of next 2 rows.
Dec one st at each end of next row, then every other row 2(3,4) times — 60(66,72) sts.

Next Row: K 2(0,5) inc in next st, * k 4(4,3), inc in next st; rep from * to last 2(0,6) sts, k 2(0,6) — 72(80,88) sts.
Beg blackberry stitch pattern:
Row 1 (right side): Knit.
Row 2: Using A, k 2, *(k 1, p 1, k 1) in next st, p 3 tog; rep from * to last 2 sts, k 2.
Row 3: Purl.
Row 4: Using B, k 2, * p 3 tog, (k 1, p 1, k 1) in next st; rep from * to last 2 sts, k 2.
Row 5: Purl.
Row 6: Using Mc, rep Row 2.
Row 7: Purl.
Row 8: Using A, rep Row 4.
Row 9: Purl.
Row 10: Using B, rep Row 2.
Row 11: Purl.
Row 12: Using Mc, rep Row 4.
Row 13: Purl.
Rep Rows 2 to 13 for blackberry stitch pattern.
Work 17(17,19) rows in pat.
Bind off loosely.
LEFT FRONT
Using No. 1 needles and Mc, cast on 34(42,46) sts.
Work 1¹/2" in rib as for lower band of Back, ending with Row 2 and inc 3(0,0) sts evenly across last row — 37(42,46) sts.
Change to No. 3 needles.

SIZE
Directions are given for size 3 months. Changes for 6 months and 9 months are in parentheses.

MATERIALS
Fingering-Weight Yarn (50 gr. ball): 4(4,5) balls of main color (Mc), 1 ball each of blue (A) and pink (B); 1 pair each of No. 1 and No. 3 knitting needles *or any size needles to obtain gauge below*; 6 buttons; tapestry needle.

GAUGE
On No. 3 needles in stockinette stitch (st st) — 8 sts = 1"; 11 rows = 1". On No. 3 needles in blackberry stitch pattern — 10 sts = 1"; 11 rows = 1". Be sure to check your gauge.

MEASUREMENTS

Sizes (mos.):	3	6	9
Body Chest:	16"	18"	20"
Finished Measurements:			
Chest:	18"	20"	22"
Length to Back Neck:			
	9"	10"	11"
Sleeve Length:			
	5¹/4"	6¹/4"	7¹/4"

Continue in st st until work measures 5¹/2(6,7)" from beg, ending with a purl row. **

Armhole and Front Neck Shaping:
Next Row: Bind off 4(5,5) sts, knit to last 2 sts, k 2 tog.

Dec one st at armhole edge every other row 3(4,5) times, **at the same time** dec one st at neck edge every other row 3(4,5) times — 26(28,30) sts.
Purl one row, inc 6(7,8) sts evenly across — 32(35,38) sts.
Beg Blackberry Stitch pat:
Row 1: Knit to last 2 sts, k 2 tog.
Row 2: Using A, k 1(0,3), * (k 1, p 1, k 1) in next st, p 3 tog; rep from * to last 2 sts, k 2.
Row 3: Purl to last 2 sts, p 2 tog.
Row 4: Using B, k 0(3,2), * p 3 tog, (k 1, p 1, k 1) in next st; rep from * to last 2 sts, k 2.
Row 5: Rep Row 3.
Row 6: Using Mc, k 3(2,1), * (k 1, p 1, k 1) in next st, p 3 tog; rep from * to last 2 sts, k 2.
Keeping in blackberry stitch pat as established in Rows 2 to 6 above, dec one st at neck edge in next row, then every other row 2(2,1) times, then every 4th row 4(4,5) times — 22(25,28) sts.
Work even for 3 rows.
Bind off loosely.
RIGHT FRONT
Work as for Left Front to **.
Armhole and Front Neck Shaping:
Next Row: K 2 tog, knit to end.
Next Row: Bind off 4(5,5) sts, purl to end.
Dec one st at armhole edge in next row, then every other row 2(3,4) times, **at the same time** dec one st at neck edge in next row, then every other row 2(3,4) times — 26(28,30) sts.
Purl one row, inc 6(7,8) sts evenly across — 32(35,38) sts.
Beg blackberry stitch pattern:
Row 1: K 2 tog, knit to end.
Row 2: Using A, k 2, * (k 1, p 1, k 1) in next st, p 3 tog; rep from * to last 1(0,3) sts, k 1(0,3).
Row 3: P 2 tog, purl to end.
Row 4: Using B, k 2, * p 3 tog, (k 1, p 1, k 1) in next st; rep from * to last 0(3,2) sts, k 0(3,2).
Row 5: Rep Row 3.
Row 6: Using Mc, k 2, * (k 1, p 1, k 1) in next st, p 3 tog; rep from * to last 3(2,1) sts, k 3(2,1).
Keeping in blackberry stitch pat as established in Rows 2 to 6 above, complete to correspond with Left Front.
SLEEVES
Using No. 1 needles and Mc, cast on 42(42,46) sts.
Work 1¹/2" in rib as for lower band of Back, ending with Row 2 and inc 6 sts evenly across last row — 48(48,52) sts.
Change to No. 3 needles.

Continue in st st, inc one st at each end of 3rd row then every 4th(4th,6th) rows until there are 54(58,58) sts, then every 6th(6th,8th) rows until there are 60(64,66) sts.

Work even in st st until length measures 5¼(6¼,7¼)" from beg, ending with a purl row.

Cap Shaping:
Bind off 2(3,3) sts at beg of next 2 rows. Dec one st at each end of next row and every other row until 44(44,40) sts rem, then in every row until 14 sts rem.
Bind off.

RIGHT FRONT BAND
Using No. 1 needles and Mc, cast on 11 sts.

Row 1: K 1, * p 1, k 1; rep from * to end.
Rep Row 1 for pat.
Work 3 rows in pat.
Row 5: Work in pat across 4 sts, bind off 2 sts, pat across 5 sts.
Row 6: Work in pat across 5 sts, cast on 2 sts, pat across 4 sts.
Work 12(14,14) rows in pat.
Rep Rows 5 and 6 once, then work 18(18,20) rows in pat.
Rep last 20(20,22) rows 3 times more, then Rows 5 and 6 once.***

Collar Shaping:
Keeping in pat as established, inc one st at end of next and every other row 4 times, then every 4th row until there are 25 sts.
Work 47(49,53) rows in pat.
Bind off loosely.

LEFT FRONT BAND
Work as for Right Front Band to ***, omitting buttonholes.

Collar Shaping:
Keeping in pat, inc one st at beg of next and foll alt rows 4 times, then every 4th row until there are 25 sts.
Work 47(49,53) rows in pat.
Bind off loosely.

FINISHING
Press lightly on wrong side with cool iron, except for collar. Sew shoulder seams, side and sleeve seams, then sew in sleeves. Sew Front Bands in place, and join seam at center back gathering extra to fit at back neck. Fold collar section in half to right side of cardigan. Sew on buttons.

BLACKBERRY STITCH BOOTIES

TECHNIQUE: Knitting

DIRECTIONS
BOOTIES
Using Mc, cast on 43 sts.
Row 1: (K 1, inc in next st, k 18, inc in next st) twice, k 1 — 47 sts.
Row 2 and All Even Numbered Rows: Knit
Row 3: (K 1, inc in next st, k 20, inc in next st) twice, k 1 — 51 sts.
Row 5: (K 1, inc in next st, k 22, inc in next st) twice, k 1 — 55 sts.
Row 7: (K 1, inc in next st, k 24, inc in next st) twice, k 1 — 59 sts.
Row 9: (K 1, inc in next st, k 26, inc in next st) twice, k 1 — 63 sts.
Row 11: (K 1, inc in next st, k 28, inc in next st) twice, k 1 — 67 sts.
Row 12: K 2 tog, k 63, k 2 tog — 65 sts.
Beg blackberry stitch pattern:
Row 1 (right side): Knit.
Row 2: Using A, k 2, *(k 1, p 1, k 1) in next st, p 3 tog; rep from * to last 3 sts, k 3.
Row 3: Purl.
Row 4: Using B, k 2, *p 3 tog, (k 1, p 1, k 1) in next st; rep from * to last 3 sts, k 3.
Row 5: Purl.
Row 6: Using Mc; rep Row 2.
Row 7: Purl.
Row 8: Using A; rep Row 4.
Row 9: Purl.

SIZE
Directions are given for Booties to fit a 3-3½" length foot.

NOTE: For slightly smaller booties, use one size smaller needles and for slightly larger booties, use one size larger needles than suggested to obtain the correct gauge.

MATERIALS
Fingering -Weight Yarn (50 gr. ball): 1 ball of main color (Mc) and 1 ball each of blue (A) and pink (B); 1 pair No. 3 knitting needles, *or any size needles to obtain gauge below;* 1 yard of ⅜"-wide ribbon; tapestry needle.

GAUGE
On No. 3 needles in stockinette stitch (st st) — 8 sts = 1"; 11 rows = 1". Be sure to check your gauge.

Row 10: Using B; rep Row 2.
Row 11: Purl.
Row 12: Using Mc; rep Row 4.
Instep Shaping:
Next Row: K 27 Mc, using A, k 10, k 2 tog, turn.
Next Row: Using A, sl 1, k 9, k 2 tog, turn.
Rep last row until 45 sts rem (17 sts on each side of instep).
Next Row: Using A, k 10, k 2 tog, using Mc, knit to end.
Next Row: Using Mc, Purl — 44 sts.
ANKLE
Next Row: K 1, *yo, k 2 tog; rep from * to last st, k 1.
Next Row: Purl, inc 1 st in center st — 45 sts.
Next Row: K 2, *p 1, k 1; rep from * to last st, k 1.
Next Row: K 1, *p 1, k 1; rep from * to end.
Rep last two rows 4 times.
Purl 2 rows.
Rep Rows 2 to 12 of blackberry stitch pattern once.
Work 3 rows garter stitch (k every row).
Bind off

FINISHING
Sew foot and back seam, reversing back seam above rib. Thread ribbon through eyelet holes of ankle, and tie in a bow as shown. Fold ankle section above rib to right side.

BABY'S BLUE AND WHITE PULLOVER AND LEGGINGS

TECHNIQUE: Knitting

DIRECTIONS
PULLOVER
BACK
Using No. 2 needles and Mc, cast on 59(67,73) sts.

Row 1: K 2, *p 1, k 1; rep from * to last st, k 1.

Row 2: K 1, *p 1, k 1; rep from * to end.

Rep Rows 1 and 2 until lower band measures 1¼(1¼,1½)" from beg, ending with Row 2.

Change to No. 4 needles and **beg pattern stitch:**

Row 1 and All Odd Numbered Rows (right side): Knit.

Row 2: K 4(8,1), p 1, * k 9, p 1; rep from * to last 4(8,1) sts, k 4(8,1).

Row 4: K 3(7,0), p 3, * k 7, p 3; rep from * to last 3(7,0) sts, k 3(7,0).

Row 6: K 2(0,0), p 5(1,4), * k 5, p 5; rep from * to last 2(6,9) sts, k 2(5, 5), p 0(1,4).

Row 8: K 1(0, 0), p 7(2,5), * k 3, p 7; rep from * to last 1(5,8) sts, k 1(3,3), p 0(2,5).

Row 10: P 9(3,6), * k 1, p 9; rep from * to last 0(4,7) sts, k 0(1,1), p 0(3, 6).

Row 12: K 9(3,6), * p 1, k 9; rep from * to last 0(4,7) sts, p 0(1,1), k 0(3,6).

Row 14: P 1(0,0), k 7(2,5), *p 3, k 7; rep from * to last 1(5,8) sts, p 1(3, 3), k 0(2,5).

Row 16: P 2(0,0), k 5(1,4), * p 5, k 5; rep from * to last 2(6,9) sts, p 2(5,5), k 0(1,4).

Row 18: P 3(0,0), k 3(0,3), *p 7, k 3; rep from * to last 3(7,0) sts, p 3(7,0).

Row 20: P4(8,1), k 1, *p 9, k 1; rep from * to last 4(8,1) sts, p 4(8,1).

Rows 1 to 20 form pattern stitch.

Continue in pat until work measures 5 (5½,6½)" from beg, working last row on wrong side.**

Divide for Back Opening:
Row 1: K 32(36,39), turn.

Continue on these 32(36,39) sts.

Row 2: K 5, work in pat to end.

Row 3: Knit.

Rep Rows 2 and 3 once, then Row 2 once.

Row 7: K 28(32,35), bind off 2 sts, k 2.

Row 8: K 2, cast on 2 sts, k 1, work in pat to end.

Keeping in pat as established, work

10(10,12) rows in garter st (k every row) across stitches at left edge.

Rep last 12(12,14) rows once, then first 6(8,8) of these 12(12,14) rows once — *3 buttonholes made.*

Shoulder Shaping:
Keeping in pat, bind off 6(7,8) sts at beg of next row and every other row once, then 7(8,9) sts at beg of every other row once. ***

Work even for 1 row.

Leave rem 13(14,14) sts on a stitch holder for center back neck.

Join yarn to rem sts at center back, cast on 5 sts and knit to end.

Row 2: Work in pat to last 5 sts, k 5.

Row 3: Knit.

Rep Rows 2 and 3 17(18,20) times.

Shoulder Shaping:
Complete as for other shoulder to ***.

Leave rem 13(14,14) sts on a stitch holder.

FRONT
Work as for Back to **.

Work 22(24,26) more rows in pat.

Neck Shaping:
Next Row: K 24(27,30), turn.

**** Keeping in pat, dec one st at neck edge every other row 5 times.

Work even for 3(3,5) rows.****

Shoulder Shaping:
Bind off 6(7,8) sts at beg of next row and every other row once.

Work even for 1 row.

Bind off.

Slip next 11(13,13) sts onto a stitch holder for front neck.

Join yarn to rem sts and knit to end.

Rep from **** to ****.

Work even for 1 row.

Shoulder Shaping:
Complete as for other shoulder.

SLEEVES
Using No. 2 needles and Mc, cast on 35(37,39) sts.

Work 1¼(1¼,1½)" in rib as for lower band of Back, ending with Row 2, and inc 12(12,14) sts evenly across last row — 47(49,53) sts.

Change to No. 4 needles and beg pat.

Continue in pat following 2nd size of Back for **1st Size of Sleeves**, 1st size of Back for **2nd Size of Sleeves**, and 3rd size of Back for **3rd Size of Sleeves**, until work measures 5½(6½,7½)" from beg, working last row on wrong side.

Cap Shaping:
Working in pat, bind off 6(6,7) sts at beg of next 6 rows.

Bind off.

NECKBAND
Sew shoulder seams. With right side facing, using No. 2 needles and Mc, pick

up and k 63(67,71) sts evenly around neck edge, including sts from stitch holders. Work 5 rows in rib as for lower band of Back, beg with Row 2.

Row 6: Rib to last 4 sts, bind off 2 sts, rib 2.

Row 7: Rib 2, cast on 2 sts, rib to end. Work 2 rows in rib.

Bind off loosely in rib.

FINISHING

Mark sides 3½(4,4½)" down from each shoulder seam on Front and Back. Sew in sleeves between markers. Sew side and sleeve seams. Sew the 5 cast-on sts at center back in place. Sew on buttons. Using duplicate stitch and A, embroider triangles on Front, beg at center about 4½" down from neck shaping and extending diagonally outwards as illustrated (see chart A).

LEGGINGS

RIGHT LEG (Beg at waist)

Using No. 2 needles and Mc, cast on 81(85,89) sts.

Row 1: K 2, *p 1, k 1; rep from * to last st, k 1.

Row 2: K 1, *p 1, k 1; rep from * to end.

Rep Rows 1 and 2 twice, inc 1 st in center of last row — 82(86,90) sts.

Change to No. 4 needles.

Work 2 rows in st st.

Back Shaping:

Note: To avoid holes when turning, bring yarn to front of work, slip next st onto right-hand needle, with yarn in back of work, sl st back onto left-hand needle, then turn and proceed as instructed. ****

Row 1: K 14(16,18) turn.

Row 2 and All Even Numbered Rows: Purl.

Row 3: K 21(23,25), turn.

Row 5: K 28(30,32), turn.

Row 7: K 35(37,39), turn.

Row 9: K 42(44,46), turn.

Continue turning in this manner, working 7 more sts every other row until the row "k 70(72,74), turn" has been worked.

Next Row: Purl.

*****Continue in st st, inc 1 st at each end of 11th then every 10th(12th,14th) row until there are 88(92, 96) sts.

Continue until shorter side edge measures 6¼(6½,7½)" from beg, ending with a purl row.

Mark end of last row for back edge.

Leg Shaping:

Dec 1 st at each end of next row and every 3rd row until 58(66,86) sts rem, then every 4th row until 56(60,64) sts rem. Continue in st st until side edge measures 6(7,8)" from marker, ending with a purl row and dec 15 sts evenly across last row — 41(45,49) sts.

Change to No. 2 needles and work 12 rows in rib as for waist, dec 1 st at end of last row — 40(44, 48) sts.

Change to No. 4 needles. *****

Divide for foot:

Row 1: K 37(40,43), turn.

Row 2: P 14, turn.

Work 14(16,18) rows on these 14 sts.

Cut yarn and slip these sts onto a stitch holder.

With right side facing, join yarn to inside edge where the 23(26, 29) sts were left, pick up and k 12(13,14) sts along side of instep, k across 14 sts on needle (inc 1 st in center), pick up and k 12(13,14) sts along other side of instep, then knit across rem 3(4,5) sts — 65(71,77) sts.

Knit 13 rows garter stitch (k every row).

GRAPH B

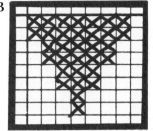

☒ A (embroidered on afterwards)

Foot Shaping:

Row 1: K 7(8,9), (k 2 tog, k 2) twice, k 25(28,31), (k 2 tog, k 1) twice, k 19(21,23) — 61(67,73) sts.

Row 2 and All Even Numbered Rows: Knit.

Row 3: K 6(7,8), (k 2 tog, k 2) twice, k 23(25,29), (k 2 tog, k 1) twice, k 18(20,22) — 57(63,69) sts.

Row 5: K 5(6,7), (k 2 tog, k 2) twice, k 21(24, 27), (k 2 tog, k 1) twice, k 17(19, 21) — 53(59, 65) sts.

Row 7: K 4(5,6), (k 2 tog, k 2) twice, k 19(22,25), (k 2 tog, k 1) twice, k 16(18, 20) — 49(55,61) sts.

Bind off.

LEFT LEG

Beg at waist, work as for Right Leg to ****.

Row 1 and All Odd Numbered Rows: Knit.

Row 2: P 14(16,18), turn.

Row 4: P 21(23,25), turn.

Row 6: P 28(30,32), turn.

Row 8: P 35(37,39), turn.

Row 10: P 42(44,46), turn.

Continue turning in this manner, working 7 sts more every other row until the row "p 70(72,74) turn" has been worked.

Work as for Right Leg from ***** to *****, mark beg of the corresponding row, instead of at the end.

Divide for foot

Row 1: K 17(18,19), turn.

Row 2: P 14, turn.

Work 14(16,18) rows on these 14 sts.

Cut yarn and slip these sts onto a stitch holder.

With right side facing, join yarn to inside edge where sts were left, pick up and k 12(13,14) sts along side of instep, k across 14 sts on needle (inc one st in center), pick up and k 12(13, 14) sts along other side of instep, then k across rem 26(30, 34) sts — 65(71,77) sts.

Knit 13 rows in garter stitch.

Foot Shaping:

Row 1: K 20(22,24), (k 2 tog, k 1) twice, k 26(29,32), (k 2 tog, k 2) twice, k 5(6,7). 61(67,73) sts.

GRAPH A

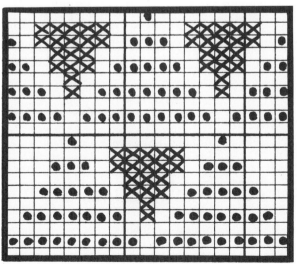

☐ K st on odd rows,
P st on even rows (MC)

⊡ K st on even rows (MC)

☒ A (embroidered on afterwards)

Row 2 and All Even Numbered Rows: Knit.

Row 3: K 19(21,23), (k 2 tog, k 1) twice, k 24(27,30), (k 2 tog, k 2) twice, k 4(5,6) — 57(63,69) sts.

Row 5: K 18(20, 22),(k 2 tog, k 1) twice, k 22(25,28), (k 2 tog, k 2) twice, k 3(4,5) — 53(59,65) sts.

Row 7: K 17(19, 21), (k 2 tog, k 1) twice, k 20(23,26), (k 2 tog, k 2) twice, k 2(3,4) — 49(55,61) sts.
Bind off.

FINISHING

Using duplicate stitch and A, embroider one triangle in center of each instep following chart B. Sew back, front, leg and foot seams. Thread elastic through 1st, 3rd, and 5th rows of rib at waist.

PINK AND WHITE BABY'S CARDIGAN

TECHNIQUE: Knitting

DIRECTIONS
BACK
Using No. 2 needles and Mc, cast on 71(77,83,89) sts.

Row 1: K 2, * p 1, k 1; rep from * to last st, k 1.

Row 2: K 1, * p 1, k 1; rep from * to end.
Rep Rows 1 and 2 until lower band measures 1¼" from beg, ending with Row 2 and inc one st at end of last row — 72(78,84,90) sts.
Change to No. 4 needles.
Using A
Work 2 rows in st st (k 1 row, p 1 row).

Beg pattern stitch:
Note: Always slip sts purlways in pattern.

Row 1: Using Mc, k 2, sl 2, * k 4, sl 2; rep from * to last 2 sts, k 2.

Row 2: K 1, p 1, sl 2, p 1, * k 2, p 1, sl 2, p 1; rep from * to last st, k 1.

Row 3: Using A, k 1, C2F, C2B, * k 2, C2F, C2B; rep from * to last st, k 1.

Row 4: Purl.
Rows 1 to 4 inclusive form pattern stitch.
Continue in pat until work measures 5(6,7,8)" from beg, working last row on wrong side.

Armhole Shaping:
Keeping in pat, bind off 5 sts at beg of next

SIZE
Directions are given for size 3 months. Changes for 6 months, 9 months and 12 months are in parentheses.

MATERIALS
Fingering-Weight Yarn (50 gr. ball): 3(3,4,4) of pink (Mc) and 2(2,3,3) balls of white (A); 1 pair each No. 2 and No. 4 knitting needles, *or any size needles to obtain gauge below*; 4(4,5,5) buttons; tapestry needle.

GAUGE
On No. 4 needles in stockinette stitch (st st) — 15 sts = 2"; 10 rows = 1". On No. 4 needles in pattern stitch — 2 patterns = 1½". Be sure to check your gauge.

MEASUREMENTS

Sizes (mos.):	3	6	9	12
Body Chest:	16"	18"	20"	22"
Finished Measurements:				
Chest:	18"	20"	22"	24"
Length to Back Neck:				
	9"	10"	12"	13½"
Sleeve Length:				
	5½"	6½"	8	9½"

STITCHES
C2F: Knit in front of 2nd st on left-hand needle, then knit in front of first st, slipping both sts off needle together.
C2B: Knit in back of 2nd st on left-hand needle, then knit in back of first st, slipping both sts off needle together.

2 rows.
Dec one st at each end of next and every other row until 52(58,64,70) sts rem.
Work 37(41,47,51) rows.

Shoulder Shaping:
Keeping in pat, bind off 7(8,9,11) sts at beg of next 2 rows, then 7(9,10,11) sts at beg of next 2 rows.
Bind off rem 24(24,26,26) sts.

LEFT FRONT
Using No. 2 needles and Mc, cast on 35(37,41,43) sts.
Work in rib as for lower band of Back, until band measures 1¼" from beg, ending with Row 2 and inc one st at end of last row — 36(38,42,44) sts.
Change to No. 4 needles.
Using A, work 2 rows in st st.
Beg pattern stitch **.

Row 1: Using Mc, k 2, sl 2, *k 4, sl 2; rep from * to last 2(4,2,4) sts, k 2(4,2,4).

Row 2: P 0(1,0,1), k 1(2,1,2), p 1, sl 2, p 1, *k 2, p 1, sl 2, p 1; rep from * to last st, k 1.

Row 3: Using A, k 1, C2F, C2B, *k 2, C2F, C2B; rep from * to last 1(3,1,3) sts, k 1(3,1,3).

Row 4: Purl.
Rows 1 to 4 form pattern stitch.
Continue in pat until work measures same as Back to underarm, ending with the same row.

Armhole and Front Neck Shaping:
Keeping in pat, bind off 5 sts at beg of next row.
Dec 1 st at armhole edge every other row 5 times, **at the same time** dec 1 st at front edge in 2nd then every 2nd(4th,4th,4th) row 2(8,11,6) times, then every 4th(6th, 6th, 6th) row until 14(17,19,22) sts rem.

Work even for 5 rows.

Shoulder Shaping:

Bind off 7(8,9,11) sts at beg of next row.

Work even for 1 row.

Bind off.

RIGHT FRONT

Work as given for Left Front to **.

Row 1: Using Mc, k 2(4,2,4), * sl 2, k 4; rep from * to last 4 sts, sl 2, k 2.

Row 2: K 1, p 1, sl 2, p 1, * k 2, p 1, sl 2, p 1; rep from * to last 1(3,1,3) sts, k 1(2,1,2), p 0(1,0,1).

Row 3: Using A, k 1(3,1,3), * C2F, C2B, k 2; rep from * to last 5 sts, C2F, C2B, k 1.

Row 4: Purl.

Rows 1 to 4 form pattern stitch.

Continue in pat, until work measures same as Back to underarm, working last row on right side.

Armhole and Front Neck Shaping:

Keeping in pat, bind off 5 sts at beg of next row.

Dec one st at armhole edge in next row, then every other row 4 times, **at the same time** dec one st at front edge in next row, then every other 2nd(4th,4th,4th) row

2(8,11,6) times, then every 4th(6th,6th,6th) row until 14(17,19,22) sts rem.

Work even for 6 rows.

Shoulder Shaping:

Complete as for other shoulder.

SLEEVES

Using No. 2 needles and Mc, cast on 37(37,39,41) sts.

Work in rib as for lower band of Back until band measures 1¼" from beg, ending with Row 2 and inc 5(5,9,7) sts evenly across last row — 42(42,48,48) sts.

Change to No. 4 needles.

Work in pat as for Back, inc one st at each end of 5th, then every 6th(8th,10th,12th) row until there are 54(56,52,62) sts, **3rd size only** – then every 12th row until there are 60 sts, working extra sts in pat.

Work even in pat until length measures 5½(6½,8,9½)" from beg, working last row on wrong side.

Cap Shaping:

Keeping in pat, bind off 3 sts at beg of next 2 rows.

Dec 1 st at each end of next row.

Work even for 1(3,3,3) rows.

Dec 1 st at each end of next row then every other row until 14 sts rem.

Work even for 1 row. Bind off.

FRONT BAND

Sew shoulder seams.

Using No. 2 needles, cast on 11 sts.

Row 1: K 2, (p 1, k 1), 4 times, k 1.

Row 2: K 1, (p 1, k 1), 5 times.

Rep Rows 1 and 2 once.

Row 5: Rib 5, bind off 2 sts, rib 4.

Row 6: Rib 4, cast on 2 sts, rib 5.

Work 18(20,18,22) rows in rib.

Rep last 20(22,20,24) rows 2(2,3,3) times, then Rows 5 and 6 once — *4(4,5,5) buttonholes made.*

Continue in rib without buttonholes until band is length required to fit (slightly stretched) along fronts and across back of neck.

Bind off loosely in rib.

FINISHING

Sew side and sleeve seams. Sew in Sleeves. Sew Front Band in place. Sew on buttons.

WHITE PANTS WITH CONTRAST CUFFS

TECHNIQUE: Knitting

SIZE: 6 to 12 months

MATERIALS

- ⅝ yards of 39"-wide fabric
- ¼ yard of 39"-wide contrast fabric
- ⅝ yard of ½"-wide elastic

NOTE: Seam ⅜" deep with the pieces pinned right sides together. To "cut a pair," pin the pattern to doubled fabric.

DIRECTIONS

Pattern outline ▬ ▬ ▬ ▬ ▬ ▬

1 Pattern: From the full-size No. 20 pants pattern (see pullout page and pattern outline above), trace the lower pant leg, from ½" above the cuff line (20A) to the bottom and side edges: label the pattern "leg facing." Now trace half the No. 20

pattern from back edges to the side seamline (down center of the pattern); then add a seam allowance ⅜" outside the traced line; label the pattern "back pants" and label back edge. Repeat the procedure from the front edges to the side seamline and label the pattern "front pants."

2 Cutting: Cut 1 pair each of back pants and of front pants. From contrast fabric cut 1 pair of cuff facings and four 1¼"-wide piping strips, two 18" long and two 12" long.

3 Side Seams: Fold 18" piping strip in half with wrong side facing and raw edges

even. Press. Baste it to the long side seam of each front pant piece with right sides together and raw edges even. Seam a back pant piece at the long piped edge. Repeat.

4 Inner Leg Seams: Baste piping (as in Step 3) to each bottom leg edge. Fold a pants piece in half, right sides facing to bring the inner leg edges together; stitch, then press seam open. Repeat.

5 Leg Facing: Seam the short ends of a leg facing together. Pull it over a leg edge, right sides together, with its seam matching the inner leg seam. Stitch the lower edges together. Turn the facing to the inside. Turn under its raw edge and hem it to the leg. Turn the facing to the right side to make a cuff.

6 Crotch Seam: With right sides facing, pin left leg to right leg at the back seam and, again, at the front seam with inner leg seams matching. Stitch the crotch seam from top to back edge; press seam open.

7 Waist: Overcast the top edge with zigzag stitch. Turn it to ¾" to the inside and press. Stitch the finished edge, leaving small opening. Insert elastic through the hem casing, adjust its length and stitch the ends securely together.

SUNSUIT WITH BUNNY APPLIQUE

(See photograph of Sunsuit and Sunhat on page 24 - lower right)

TECHNIQUE: Sewing

SIZE: 0 to 6 months

MATERIALS
- ☐ 7/8 yard of 45"-wide cotton fabric
- ☐ 4"-square of pink fabric
- ☐ 4"-square of lightweight iron-on interfacing
- ☐ 11 hammer-on snap fasteners
- ☐ 1 yard of 3/8"-wide elastic
- ☐ tracing paper
- ☐ sewing thread to match fabric

NOTE: The sunsuit is a fully lined, one-piece garment, snapped at bloomer sides and center front. To "cut a pair," pin the pattern to folded fabric. Seam 3/8" deep with the pieces pinned right sides together.

DIRECTIONS
Pattern outline ●●●●●●●●●●●●●●●●●●
1   Pattern: Trace the full size patterns, Nos. 5 and 6 (see pullout sheet and pattern outline above) including all marks (circles, dots, "on fold," notches, A and B, front centerline). Also trace the bunny below (to match the direction shown, turn the tracing over).
2   Cutting: Cut 2 pairs of #5 upper fronts and, with the long CB/CF centerline on a fold of fabric, two #6 back and bloomers. Half of these are lining pieces.
3   Appliqué: Iron interfacing to wrong side of pink square and trace the bunny on it. Pin the square to the right front of the sunsuit with bunny placed as shown in the photograph on page 24. Work a narrow zigzag stitch on bunny outlines. With small scissors trim off excess fabric close to the stitching. Stitch again with a wider zigzag.
4   Lining: Seam upper fronts to the back and bloomers piece at the shoulder edges. Repeat for lining. Pin suit to lining, right sides together, and stitch around all edges except at the straight bottom (waist) edge. Clip to the black dot at each underarm and clip the curved edges. Turn right side out

and press. Edgestitch.
5   Leg Casing: From A to B stitch 1/8" from the edge of each leg opening. Stitch again 1/2" away to make a casing. Insert 12"-long elastic into each casing and stitch 2 or 3 times across each end.
6   Waist Casing: Pin the raw edges together and overcast them with machine zigzag. Turn the edge 5/8" to the wrong side, press, and stitch the casing. Insert 7" of elastic through the casing and pin both ends. Smooth out the fabric at each end and stitch 2 or 3 times through the elastic 5/8" from a side edge. Pull out the elastic ends and trim off the excess. Stitch the casing ends closed.
7   Snaps: Following the manufacturer's directions, apply 3 snaps to the front (at the 3 circles) and at the bloomer sides (at the 3 lower circles). Then apply 1 snap at the side of each front (under the arm) to meet the top circle above the bloomer closing.

BABY'S SUNHAT
MATERIALS
- ☐ 5/8 yard of 45"-wide poplin
- ☐ 1/4 yard of 45"-wide iron-on interfacing

NOTE: Seam 3/8" deep with pieces pinned right sides together.

DIRECTIONS
Pattern outline — ●●● — ●●● grey
1   Pattern: Trace the full pattern, Nos. 21 and 22 (see pullout sheet and pattern outline above) including grainlines and Front and Back labels.
2   Cutting: Matching the grainlines to the fabric's lengthwise grain (selvedge), cut six #21 crowns and four #22 brims. From interfacing, also cut four brims.
3   Interfacing: Iron interfacing to wrong side of each brim piece.
4   Brim: Seam 2 brim pieces together at the back edges, then at the front edges. Repeat for the brim facing. Baste brim to brim facing at the outer raw edges. Starting at the brim edge, make a continuous row of stitching, about 1/4" apart, around and around the brim, stopping 1/2" from the raw edges.
5   Crown: Seam 3 crown sections together. Repeat. Then sew the 2 half crowns together.
6   Assembly: Pin the brim to the crown, right sides together, matching a crown seam to the brim seams. Stitch 3/8" from edges. Zigzag stitch over the raw edges; turn them upward and baste. Topstitch through all layers about 1/4" above the brim seam.
7   Trim: Make a narrow fabric bow or cover a button to sew at the crown center.

PATCHWORK PILLOW

TECHNIQUE: Sewing

For this pillow, we used a preprinted patchwork fabric to make it extra quick and easy. If you prefer, piece together your own appliquéd patchwork pillow from fabric scraps.

MATERIALS

- ☐ 13" square of quilted fabric for pillow top
- ☐ 13" x 14" fabric for pillow back
- ☐ 4" x 96" fabric strip (pieced as needed) for ruffle
- ☐ 13" square each of muslin and synthetic batting
- ☐ 12" knife-edge pillow form
- ☐ 10" zipper
- ☐ 2³/₄ yards of cotton lace edging
- ☐ 1¹/₂ yards purchased piping
- ☐ quilting thread and needle
- ☐ sewing thread
- ☐ embroidery hoop (optional)

DIRECTIONS

1 Pillow Top: With edges even, baste batting to wrong side of pillow top, then muslin to back of batting, with edges even. Fasten the piece in an embroidery hoop if you like. With quilting thread, sew a small running stitch around the fabric's printed motifs through all 3 layers.

2 Piping: Starting at one corner, stitch piping to pillow top with right sides together and the stitchline ¹/₂" from the raw edges of the quilted piece. Clip the piping seam at each corner in order to turn.

3 Ruffle: Seam the short ends of the ruffle. With right sides together, stitch lace to one raw edge of the ruffle; press the lace outward and topstitch close to the seam. Starting at the seam, divide the ruffle into quarters and mark them. Sew a gathering row (the longest machine stitch) ¹/₂" from the raw edge, starting anew at each quarter. Pin ruffle, right sides together and raw edges even, to pillow top with a quarter-mark at each corner. Pull up the gathering to fit, with a little extra fullness at each corner. Stitch along the gathering row.

4 Pillow Back: Cut pillow back fabric in half to make a pair of pieces 13" x 7". At one long (center) edge of each, stitch a ¹/₂"-wide seam for 1¹/₂" at each end. In between, press a ¹/₂" seam allowance and

apply them to a zipper. Open zipper for a few inches, for turning.

5 Assembly: Pin pillow back to pillow front (over the ruffle) with right sides together and raw edges even. Stitch ¹/₂" from all 4 edges. Turn it right side out through the zipper opening. Insert pillow form and close zipper.

BUNNY SHEET

TECHNIQUE: Sewing

MATERIALS

- ☐ 1³/₄ yards of 45"-wide fine white cotton
- ☐ 6-strand embroidery cotton and needle
- ☐ a small embroidery hoop (optional)
- ☐ dressmaker's carbon
- ☐ a dry ballpoint
- ☐ white sewing thread

DIRECTIONS

1 Hem: At a short (top) edge of the fabric, turn under 5" to the wrong side and baste the raw edge, then the fold.

2 Pattern: Trace the bunny on page 32. You can face him in the opposite direction instead, by just turning over the tracing.

3 Transfer: Centered on the top edge, pin the tracing against the right side of the sheet with the top edge of the ear ¹/₂" from the fold. Slide dressmaker's carbon under the paper and trace the bunny with a dry ballpoint pen. Repeat bunny tracings across the sheet, leaving 4" between them.

4 Embroidery: With 2 strands of embroidery cotton in the needle, work continuous chain stitches over the bunny outlines. The stitching will look best if you first engage the fabric in an embroidery hoop.

5 Hem: Fold the embroidered edge over again 5" to the wrong side. Edgestitch, to make a double hem. When you make the bed, fold the embroidered edge in a deep hem over the blanket. Stitch a narrow hem at the 3 raw edges.

Trim a large square of net with wide lace and ribbons for a really pretty mosquito net.

Sleepy Time

Your baby will always have sweet dreams tucked in this lovely set of matching sheets, crib bumper and "snug as a bug" knitted blanket. The secret is all in the combination of colors and patterns. Add a sleepsuit, trimmed to match, and a delightfully cozy, knitted sleeping bag for those extra-chilly nights.

FAIR ISLE
CRIB BLANKET

TECHNIQUE: Knitting

DIRECTIONS
Using No. 6 needles and Mc, cast on 161 sts.
Beg Fair Isle Pattern:
Row 1: K 4 Mc, *k 3 A, k 3 Mc; rep from * to last st, k 1 Mc.
Row 2: P 4 Mc, * p 3 A, p 3 Mc; rep from * to last st, k 1 Mc.
Rows 3 and 4: Rep Rows 1 and 2 once.
Rows 5-8: Rep Rows 1 and 2 twice, using A in place of Mc, and Mc in place of A.
Rep Rows 1 to 8 once.
Row 17: K 4 Mc, k 3 A, k 3 Mc, k 3 A, k 3 B, * k 3 Mc, k 3 B; rep from * to last 13 sts, k 3 A, k 3 Mc, k 3 A, k 4 Mc.
Row 18: P 4 Mc, p 3 A, p 3 Mc, p 3 A, p 3 B, * p 3 Mc, p 3 B; rep from * to last 13 sts, p 3 A, p 3 Mc, p 3 A, p 4 Mc.
Rows 19 and 20: Rep last 2 rows once.
Row 21: K 4 A, k 3 Mc, k 3 A, k 3 Mc, k 3 B, *k 3 Mc, k 3 B; rep from * to last 13 sts, k 3 Mc, k 3 A, k 3 Mc, k 4 A.
Row 22: P 4 A, p 3 Mc, p 3 A, p 3 Mc, p 3 B, * p 3 Mc, p 3 B; rep from * to last 13 sts, p 3 Mc, p 3 A, p 3 Mc, p 4 A.
Rows 23 and 24: Rep last 2 rows once.
Row 25: K 4 Mc, k 3 A, k 3 Mc, k 3 A, * k 8 C, k 1 Mc; rep from * to last 13 sts, k 3 A, k 3 Mc, k 3 A, k 4 Mc.
Row 26: P 4 Mc, p 3 A, p 3 Mc, p 3 A, * p 2 Mc, p 7 C; rep from * to last 13 sts, p 3 A, p 3 Mc, p 3 A, p 4 Mc.
Row 27: K 4 Mc, k 3 A, k 3 Mc, k 3 A, * k 6 C, k 3 Mc; rep from * to last 13 sts, k 3 A, k 3 Mc, k 3 A, k 4 Mc.
Row 28: P 4 Mc, p 3 A, p 3 Mc, p 3 A, * p 4 Mc, p 5 C; rep from * to last 13 sts, p 3 A, p 3 Mc, p 3 A, p 4 Mc.
Row 29: K 4 A, k 3 Mc, k 3 A, k 3 Mc, * k 4 C, k 5 C; rep from * to last 13 sts, k 3 Mc, k 3 A, k 3 Mc, k 4 A.
Row 30: P 4 A, p 3 Mc, p 3 A, p 3 Mc, *p 6 Mc, p 3 C; rep from * to last 13 sts, p 3 Mc, p 3 A, p 3 Mc, p 4 A.
Row 31: K 4 A, k 3 Mc, k 3 A, k 3 Mc, * k 2 C, k 7 Mc; rep from * to last 13 sts, k 3 Mc, k 3 A, k 3 Mc, k 4 A.
Row 32: P 4 A, p 3 Mc, p 3 A, p 3 Mc, * p

SIZE
Size: 25" x 39"

MATERIALS
Sport-Weight Yarn (50 gr. ball): 9 balls of white (Mc), 3 balls of blue (A), 1 ball each of apricot (B), lilac (C) and coral (D); 1 pair each No. 5 and No. 6 knitting needles, *or any size needles to obtain gauge below;* length of batting about 24" x 39"; tapestry needle.

GAUGE
On No. 5 needles in stockinette stitch (st st) — 13 sts = 2"; 9 rows = 1". On No. 6 needles in pattern stitch — 13 sts = 2"; 9 rows = 1". Be sure to check your gauge.

NOTE: When changing colors, pick up new color from under the color being used, twisting yarns on wrong side of work to prevent holes. Carry color not in use loosely across wrong side of work to end of row, being careful to maintain gauge.

8 Mc, p 1 C; rep from * to last 13 sts, p 3 Mc, p 3 A, p 3 Mc, p 4 A.
Rep Rows 1-8 twice.
Rep Rows 25 to 32 once, keeping colors as established in border pat, but use D in place of Mc, and Mc in place of C for triangle pattern.
Rep Rows 17 to 24 once.
Last 64 rows form pattern stitch.
Continue in pat until work measures about 39" from beg, ending with Row 8 or Row 40.
Using Mc, work in st st (k 1 row, p 1 row) until Mc section measures same as Fair Isle pattern section, ending with a purl row. Bind off loosely.

FINISHING
Fold knitting in half (foldline is at end of Fair Isle pat section), so that right sides are together. Sew 2 sides together and turn inside out. Place batting inside and slipstitch rem side closed. Using 2 strands of A and small even running stitches, sew around inside of border, through all 3 thicknesses (including batting).

Fair Isle Crib Blanket

BABY'S SLEEPING BAG

TECHNIQUE: Knitting

DIRECTIONS
BACK
Using No. 4 needles and B, cast on 81(85,93) sts.
Row 1: K 2, * p 1, k 1; rep from * to last st, k 1.
Row 2: K 1, * p 1, k 1; rep from * to end.
Rep Rows 1 and 2 once.
Row 5: Rib 5(7,6), * yo, work 2 tog, rib 12(12,14); rep from * to last 6(8,7) sts, yo, work 2 tog, rib 4(6,5) — *6 buttonholes.*
Row 6: Rep Row 2.
Rep Rows 1 and 2 until lower band measures 4" from beg, ending with Row 2 and inc one st at end of last row — 82(86,94) sts.
Change to No. 7 needles.
Note: When changing colors, pick up new color from under the color being used, twisting yarns on wrong side to prevent

holes in work. Carry colors not in use loosely across wrong side of work to end of row.

Using Mc, work 2 rows in st st (k 1 row, p 1 row).

**Using A, work 2 rows in st st.

Using Mc, work 2 rows in st st.

Row 7: K 2 Mc, * k 2 B, k 2 Mc; rep from * to end.

Row 8: P 2 Mc, * p 2 B, p 2 Mc; rep from * to end.

Work 6 rows in st st, in stripes of 2 rows Mc, 2 rows C and 2 rows Mc**.

Beg pattern:

Row 1: K 2 Mc, k 2 A, k 2 Mc; rep from * to end.

Row 2: P 2 Mc, * p 2 A, p 2 Mc; rep from * to end.

Using Mc, work 2 rows in st st.

Row 5: K 2 B, * k 2 Mc, k 2 B; rep from * to end.

Row 6: P 2 B, * p 2 Mc, p 2 B; rep from * to end.

Using Mc, work 2 rows in st st.

Row 9: K 2 Mc, * k 2 C, k 2 Mc; rep from * to end.

Row 10: P 2 Mc, * p 2 C, p 2 Mc; rep from * to end.

Using Mc, work 2 rows in st st.

Row 13: K 2 A, * k 2 Mc, k 2 A; rep from * to end.

Row 14: P 2 A, * p 2 Mc, p 2 A; rep from * to end.

Using Mc, work 2 rows in st st.

Row 17: K 2 Mc, * k 2 B, k 2 Mc; rep from * to end.

Row 18: P 2 Mc, * p 2 B, p 2 Mc; rep from * to end.

Using Mc, work 2 rows in st st.

Row 21: K 2 C, * k 2 Mc, k 2 C; rep from * to end.

Row 22: P 2 C, * p 2 Mc, p 2 C; rep from * to end.

Using Mc, work 2 rows in st st.

Last 24 rows form pattern stitch.

Continue in pat, dec 1 st at each end of next, then every 6th(10th,10th) row until 70(78,86) sts rem, **2nd and 3rd sizes only** — then every 8th row until (76,82) sts rem. Work even in pat without shaping until work measures 16(17,18)" from beg, ending with Mc and working last row on wrong side.

Armhole Shaping:

Rows 1 and 2: Using A, bind off 10(11,12) sts at beg of next 2 rows — 50(54,58) sts.

Rows 3 and 4: Using Mc, work 2 rows in st st.

Row 5: K 2 B, * k 2 Mc, k 2 B; rep from * to end.

Row 6: P 2 B, * p 2 Mc, p 2 B; rep from *

SIZE
Directions are given for size 3 months. Changes for 6 months and 9 months are in parentheses.

MATERIALS
Sport-Weight Yarn (50 gr. ball): 5(5,6) balls of blue (Mc), 1(2,2) balls of yellow (A), 2 balls of apricot (B), 1(1,2) balls of aqua (C); 1 pair each No. 4 and No. 7 knitting needles, *or any size needles to obtain gauge below*; 18(20,20)" open-ended zipper; 6 buttons; a stitch holder; tapestry needle.

GAUGE
On No. 7 needles in pattern stitch — 11 sts = 2"; 8 rows = 1". Be sure to check your gauge.

MEASUREMENTS

Sizes (mos.):	3	6	9
Body Chest:	16"	18"	20"
Finished Measurements:			
Length to Back Neck:			
	19"	21"	22½"
Sleeve Length:			
	5½"	6½"	8"

NOTE: Garment has been designed to fit loosely.

to end.

Using Mc, work 2 rows in st st.

Using C, work 2 rows in st st.

Using Mc, work 2 rows in st st, dec once in center of last row — 49(53, 57) sts.

Now work as follows for chart (see page 38):

Row 1: K 0(0,2) Mc, k 0(1,1) A, k 1(2,2) Mc, * k 3 A, k 2 Mc, k 1A, k 1 Mc, k 3 A, k 5 Mc, k 3 A, k 1 Mc, k 1 A, k 2 Mc*; rep from * to * once, k 3 A, k 1(2,2) Mc, k 0(1,1) A, k 0(0,2) Mc.

Row 2: P 0(0,2) Mc, p 0(2,2) A, p 2 Mc, p 1A *, p 2 Mc, (p 2 A, p 2 Mc) twice, p 1 A, p 2 Mc, (p 2 A, p 2 Mc) twice p 1 A*; rep from * to * once, p 2 Mc, p 0(2,2) A, p 0(0,2) Mc.

Work Rows 3 to 21 following chart on page 38.

Using Mc work 3 rows in st st, inc one st in center of last row — 50(54,58) sts.

Using C work 2 rows in st st.

Using Mc work 2 rows in st st, **2nd and 3rd Sizes only** — Rep Rows 5 and 6 as given for armhole shaping.

3rd Size only — Using Mc work 4 rows in st st.

Shoulder Shaping: (all sizes)

Using Mc only, bind off 8(9,9) sts at beg of next 2 rows, then 8(9,10) sts at beg of next 2 rows.

Leave rem 18(18,20) sts on stitch holder for back neck.

LEFT FRONT

Using No. 4 needles and B, cast on 41(43,49) sts.

Work 6 rows in rib as for lower band of Back, inc (inc, dec) one st in center of last row. 42(44,48) sts.

Change to No. 7 needles.

Rows 1 and 2: Using Mc, work 2 rows in st st.

Rows 3 and 4: Using A, work 2 rows in st st.

Rows 5 and 6: Using Mc, work 2 rows in st st ***.

Row 7: * K 2 Mc, k 2 B; rep from * to last 2(0,0) sts, k 2(0,0) Mc.

Row 8: P 2(0, 0) Mc, *p 2 B, p 2 Mc; rep from * to end.

Work 6 rows in st st, in stripes of 2 rows Mc, 2 rows C and 2 rows Mc.

Beg pattern stitch:

Row 1: * K 2 Mc, k 2 A; rep from * to last 2(0,0) sts, k 2(0,0) Mc.

Row 2: P 2(0,0) Mc, *p 2 A, p 2 Mc; rep from * to end.

Work 22 rows more in pat (as for Back) as

Baby's Sleeping Bag

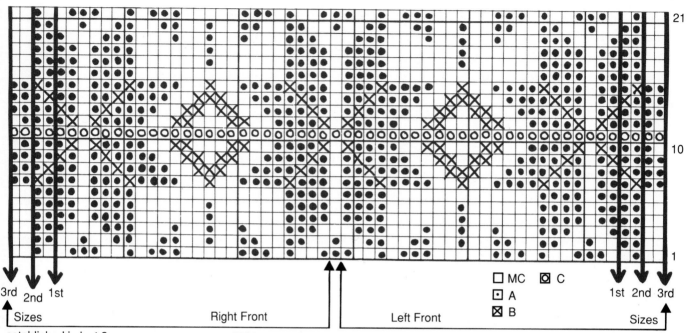

21

10

1

3rd 2nd 1st
Sizes   Right Front   Left Front

	MC		C
	A		
	B		

1st 2nd 3rd
Sizes

established in last 2 rows.
Continue in pat dec one st at beg of next row, then every 6th(10th,10th) row until 36(40,44) sts rem, **2nd and 3rd sizes only** – then every 8th row until (39,42) sts rem. Work even in pat until length of side edge measures 14(15,16)" from beg, working last row on wrong side.

Armhole Shaping:
Keeping in pat, bind off 10(11,12) sts at beg of next row — 26(28,30) sts.
Work 11 rows in pat as given for armhole shaping of Back, dec twice in center of last row — 24(26,28) sts.

Now work as follows for chart:
Next Row: K 0(0,2) Mc, k 0(1,1) A, k 1(2,2) Mc, work as given from * to * on Row 1 of Back ending with k 1 A.
Next Row: Work as given from * to * on Row 2 of Back, p 2 Mc, p 0(2,2) A, p 0(0,2) Mc.
Work Rows 3 to 15(15,19) following chart on page 38.

Neck Shaping:
Continuing to follow chart, bind off 4 sts at beg of next row — 20(22,24) sts.
Dec one st at neck edge in next row and every other row 2(2,0) times and **at the same time** complete chart — 17(19,23) sts.
Continue in pat as for Back, dec one st at neck edge every other row until 16(18,19) sts rem.
Work 5(7,5) rows in pat.

Shoulder Shaping:
Bind off 8(9,9) sts at beg of next row.
Work even for 1 row.
Bind off.

RIGHT FRONT
Work as for Left Front to ***
Row 7: K 2(0,2) Mc, * k 2 B, k 2 Mc; rep from * to end.
Row 8: * P 2 Mc, p 2 B; rep from * to last 2(0,2) sts, p 2(0,2) Mc.
Work to correspond with Left Front.

SLEEVES
Using No. 4 needles and A, cast on 31(33,35) sts.
Work as for lower band of Back until band measures 1¹/₂" from beg, ending with a Row 1.
Next Row: Inc once in each st to end — 62(66,70) sts.
Change to No. 7 needles and Mc.
Work in pat st (as for Back), until work measures about 5¹/₄(6¹/₄,7¹/₂)" from beg, ending with a purl row in Mc.
Mark each end of last row for beg of armhole.
Work as given from ** to ** on Back.
Using Mc, work 2(4,6) rows in st st.

Cap Shaping:
Bind off 8 sts at beg of next 6 rows.
Bind off rem sts.

NECKBAND
Sew shoulder seams. With right side facing, using No. 4 needles and Mc, pick up and k 53(57,59) sts evenly around neck (including sts from stitch holder).
Work in rib as for lower band of Back, beg with Row 2, until neckband measures 1¹/₄" from beg, ending with Row 2.
Bind off loosely in rib.

FINISHING
Press lightly on wrong side, using a damp

cloth and cool iron. Sew side and sleeve seams up to markers. Sew in sleeves, matching markers of sleeves to bound-off sts at armholes. Sew in zipper. Fold lower band edge onto right side of Front. Sew on buttons to correspond with buttonholes.

FAIR ISLE

Fair Isle is a small island off the coast of Scotland, which has given its name to a very easily recognizable colored knitting pattern. Local legend has it that the colors and intricate patterns were based on those worn by Spanish sailors shipwrecked on the island after the defeat of the Spanish Armada in 1588. Others hold that the patterns were handed down by Viking explorers from Scandinavia.

A true Fair Isle pattern usually had two colors to a row and used a Shetland wool called "fingering." In the past the lovely colors of Fair Isle were dyed with natural dyes. These days chemical dyes are used to reproduce traditional colors. Classic Fair Isle patterns have been repeated unchanged for generations.

SHEET WITH STRIPED BORDER

TECHNIQUE: Sewing

This sheet is made just like the Sheet with Dotted Border on page 23. We have edged plain cotton fabric with a pretty striped border pattern in varying shades of cream and apricot. The bias trim can be a complementary or contrasting color.

CREAM PAJAMAS

TECHNIQUE: Sewing

Make this cozy pajama suit, following the directions for the Striped Pajama suit on page 23. We have used stretch terry cloth, trimmed with bias made from the Crib Bumper fabric. Stretch terry is comfortable for baby and so easy to care for.

CRIB BUMPER

TECHNIQUE: Sewing
MATERIALS
The amount of fabric required depends on the size of your crib.
☐ Cotton or polyester/cotton fabric : one piece the width of the crib by twice the distance from the mattress to the top rail; two pieces two thirds the length of the crib by twice the distance from the mattress to the top rail
☐ scraps of fabric, ribbon or doubled bias tape for ties
☐ thin synthetic batting in same size as fabric
☐ sewing thread to match fabric
DIRECTIONS
1 Sew batting to wrong side of each fabric piece. Fold each piece in half with right sides together. Sew around edges, leaving opening for turning. Turn to right side. Slipstitch opening closed.
2 Make 12 ties each ³/₄" x 32". Stitch center of each tie to each corner of three bumper sections. Topstitch all around each bumper section 1" from edge to finish.

Above top: Sheet with Striped Border, Crib Bumper; Above: Cream Pajamas

Lavender and Lace

You can almost smell the fresh lavender! Pastel purples and greens lend themselves
beautifully to baby's layette. Team the lacy knitted ensemble in snowy white
with the prettiest lavender, green and white patchwork quilt. Tuck baby in for the night
in an angelic embroidered nightie made from gossamer voile.

JACKET, BONNET AND BOOTIES

TECHNIQUE: Knitting

DIRECTIONS
JACKET
BACK

Using No. 3 needles, cast on 146(162,178) sts.

Work 3 rows in garter st (k every row), (Row 1 is wrong side).

Beg pattern stitch:

Row 1 (right side): P 2, *k 4, k 2 tog, yo, p 2; rep from * to end.

Row 2: K 2, * yo, p 1, p 2 tog, p 3, k 2; rep from * to end.

Row 3: P 2, *k 2, k 2 tog, k 2, yo, p 2; rep from * to end.

Row 4: K 2, * yo, p 3, p 2 tog, p 1, k 2; rep from * to end.

Row 5: P 2, *k 2 tog, k 4, yo, p 2; rep from * to end.

Row 6: K 2, *p 4, p 2 tog, yo, k 2; rep from * to end.

Row 7: P 2, * yo, k 1, k 2 tog, k 3, p 2; rep from * to end.

Row 8: K 2, *p 2, p 2 tog, p 2, yo, k 2; rep from * to end.

Row 9: P 2, * yo, k 3, k 2 tog, k 1, p 2; rep from * to end.

Row 10: K 2, *p 2 tog, p 4, yo, k 2; rep from * to end.

Rows 1 to 10 form pattern stitch.

Continue in pat until work measures 6¹/2(7,8¹/2)" from beg, working last row on wrong side.

Next Row: K 1, *k 2 tog; rep from * to last st, k 1 — 74(82,90) sts.

Next Row: Purl.

Next Row: K 2(1,2), * yo, k 2 tog, k 1; rep from * to last 0(0,1) sts, k 0(01).

Work 3 rows in st st (k 1 row, p 1 row), beg with a purl row.

Armhole Shaping:

Bind off 4(4,5) sts at beg of next 2 rows.

Dec 1 st at each end of next and every other row until 60(66,72) sts rem.

Work even for 31(31,35) rows.

Shoulder Shaping:

Bind off 10(11,12) sts at beg of next 2 rows, then 9(10,11) sts at beg of next 2 rows.

Leave rem 22(24,26) sts on a stitch holder for back neck.

SIZE

Directions are given for size 3 months. Changes for 6 months and 9 months are in parenttheses.

MATERIALS

Fingering-Weight Yarn (50 gr. ball): 3(3,4) balls for Jacket, 1 ball each for Bonnet and Booties; 1 pair each No. 1 and No. 3 knitting needles, *or any size needles to obtain gauge below*; 3 stitch holders for Jacket; length of ribbon; tapestry needle.

GAUGE

On No. 3 needles in stockinette stitch (st st) — 8 sts = 1"; 11 rows = 1". Be sure to check your gauge.

MEASUREMENTS

Sizes (mos.):	3	6	9
Body Chest:	16"	18"	20"
Finished Measurements:			
Chest:	18"	20"	22"
Length to Back Neck:			
	10¹/2"	11¹/2"	13"
Sleeve Length:			
	5"	6"	7"

STITCHES

M1: Pick up loop which lies before next st, place it on left-hand needle, and knit through back of loop. This increases a stitch.

LEFT FRONT

Using No. 3 needles, cast on 80(88,96) sts.

Work 3 rows in garter st (Row 1 is wrong side). **

Beg pattern stitch:

Row 1 (right side): P 2, * k 4, k 2 tog, yo, p 2; rep from * to last 6 sts, k 6.

Row 2: K 6, * k 2 yo, p 1, p 2 tog, p 3; rep from * to last 2 sts, k 2.

Continue in pat as for Back (working garter st border as established in last 2 rows) until work measures 6¹/2(7,8¹/2)" from beg, working last row on wrong side.

Next Row: * K 2 tog; rep from * to last 6 sts, k 6 — 43(47,51) sts.

Next Row: K 6, purl to end.

Next Row: K 1(2,0), * k 1, yo, k 2 tog; rep from * to last 6 sts, k 6.

Continue in st st for 3 rows (beg with a purl row), working garter st border as established.

Armhole Shaping:

Bind off 4(4,5) sts at beg of next row.

Dec 1 st at armhole edge every other row until 36(39,42) sts rem.

Work even for 16(16,18) rows.

Neck Shaping:

Row 1: Work in pat across 11(12,12) sts and slip them onto a stitch holder for front neck, purl to end.

Continue on these 25(27, 30) sts.

Dec 1 st at end (neck edge) of next and every other row until 19(21,23) sts rem.

Work even for 3 rows.

Shoulder Shaping:

Bind off 10(11,12) sts at beg of next row.

Work even for 1 row.

Bind off.

RIGHT FRONT

Work as for Left Front to **.

Beg pattern stitch:

Row 1: K 6, p 2, *k 4, k 2 tog, yo, p 2; rep from * to end.

Row 2: K 2, * yo, p 1, p 2 tog, p 3, k 2; rep from * to last 6 sts, k 6.

Work to correspond with Left Front.

SLEEVES

Using No. 1 needles, cast on 43(45,47) sts.

Row 1: K 2, *p 1, k 1; rep from * to last st, k 1.

Row 2: K 1, *p 1, k 1; rep from * to end.

Rep Row 1 and 2, 6 times.

Change to No. 3 needles.

Next Row: K 6(5,2), *inc in next st, k 1; rep from * to last 5(4,1) sts, k 5(4,1) — 59(63, 69) sts.

Continue in st st (beg with a purl row) until work measures 5(6,7)" from beg, ending with a purl row.

Cap Shaping:

Bind off 2(2,3) sts at beg of next 2 rows.

Dec 1 st at each end of next and every other row until 47(51,55) sts rem, then in every row until 13 sts rem.

Bind off.

NECKBAND

Sew shoulder seams.

With right side facing and using No. 1 needles, pick up and k 72(78,84) sts evenly around neck (including sts from stitch holders).

Row 1 (wrong side): Knit.

Row 2: K 6, * k 1, yo, k 2 tog; rep from * to last 6 sts, k 6.

Knit 5 rows.

Bind off.

FINISHING

Press very lightly with a cool iron on wrong side if desired. Sew side and sleeve seams.

Sew in sleeves. Thread ribbon through holes at underarm and neck, as shown.

BONNET

Using No. 1 needles, cast on 90(98,106) sts.

Work 5 rows in garter st (Row 1 is wrong side).

Change to No. 3 needles.

Work 12 rows in st st.

Work 20 rows in pat, as for Back of Jacket.

Continue in st st until work measures 5 (5¼, 5½)" from beg, ending with a purl row.

Crown Shaping:

Row 1: K 1, * k 2 tog, k 9(10,11); rep from * to last st, k 1 — 82(90,98) sts.

Row 2 and All Even Numbered Rows: K 1, purl to last st, k 1.

Row 3: K 1, *k 2 tog, k 8(9, 10); rep from * to last st, k 1 — 74(82,90) sts.

Row 5: K 1, *k 2 tog, k 7(8,9); rep from * to last st, k 1 — 66(74,82) sts.

Continue to dec in this manner in every other row until 10 sts rem.

Cut yarn, pull end through rem sts, draw up and fasten off securely.

LOWER BAND

Sew crown seam.

With right side facing and using No. 1 needles, pick up and k 68(72,76) sts evenly around lower edge.

Work 3 rows in garter st.

Bind off.

FINISHING

Attach ribbons to each side of Bonnet and tie, as shown.

BOOTIES

Using No. 3 needles, cast on 35(39,43) sts.

Row 1 (wrong side): K 1, M1, k 16(18,20), M1, k 1, M1, k 16(18,20), M1, k 1 — 39(43,47) sts.

Row 2 and All Even Numbered Rows: Knit.

Row 3: K 1, M1, k 18(20, 22), M1, k 1, M1, k 18(20,22), M1,k 1 — 43(47,51) sts.

Row 5: K 1, M1, k 20(22,24), M1, k 1, M1, k 20(22,24), M1, k 1 — 47(51,55) sts.

Shawl, Jacket and Bonnet

Inc in this manner every other row until there are 59(63,67) sts.
Next Row: K 2 tog, knit to last 2 sts, k 2 tog — 57(61,65) sts.
Work 5(7,11) rows in garter st.
Instep Shaping:
Row 1: K 33(35,37), k 2 tog, turn.
Row 2: Sl 1, p 9, p 2 tog, turn.
Row 3: Sl 1, k 9, k 2 tog, turn.
Row 4: Sl 1, p 9, p 2 tog, turn.
Rep Rows 3 and 4 until 37(41,45) sts rem.
Next Row: Sl 1, k 9, k 2 tog, knit to end — 36(40,44) sts.
Next Row: Knit across all sts to end.

Next Row: K 1, * yo, k 2 tog; rep from * to last st, k 1.
Next Row: Knit, inc 6(2,6) sts evenly across row — 42(42,50) sts.
Work 20 rows in pat as for Back of Jacket, dec (inc, dec) 1 st in center of last row — 41(43,49) sts. Change to No. 1 needles and work 8 rows in rib as for Sleeves of Jacket.
Bind off loosely in rib.

FINISHING
Do not press.
Sew foot and back seam. Thread narrow ribbon through holes and tie into a bow.

BABY'S SHAWL

TECHNIQUE: Knitting

DIRECTIONS
CENTER SECTION
Using No. 3 needles, cast on 224 sts.
Row 1: * P 1, k 1; rep from * to end.
Row 2: * K 1, p 1; rep from * to end.
Last 2 rows form Moss Stitch.
Rep Rows 1 and 2, 4 times, dec 12 sts evenly across last row (but do not dec across 10 sts at each end) — 212 sts.
Beg center pattern stitch:
Row 1(right side): (P 1, k 1) 5 times, * k 3, yo, sl 1, k 2 tog, psso, yo; rep from * to last 10 sts, (p 1, k 1) 5 times.
Row 2: (K 1, p 1) 5 times, purl to last 10 sts, (k 1, p 1) 5 times.
Row 3: (P 1, k 1) 5 times, * yo, sl 1 k 2 tog, psso, yo, k 3; rep from * to last 10 sts, (p 1, k 1) 5 times.

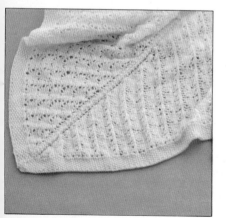

SIZE
Directions are given for a Blanket measuring 54" square.

MATERIALS
Fingering-Weight Yarn (50 gr. ball): 10 balls; 1 pair of No. 3 knitting needles, *or any size needles to obtain gauge below;* tapestry needle.

GAUGE
On No. 3 needles in stockinette stitch (st st) — 8 sts = 1"; 11 rows = 1". On No. 3 needles in center pattern stitch — 15 sts = 2"; 11 rows = 1". Be sure to check your gauge.

Row 4: Rep Row 2.
Rows 1 to 4 form center pattern st.
Continue in pat until work measures 25" from beg, working last row on wrong side and inc 12 sts evenly across last row (do not inc across 10 sts at each end) — 224 sts.
Work 10 rows in Moss Stitch.
Bind off loosely.
BORDER (make 4):
With right side facing, using No. 3 needles, pick up and k 213 sts evenly along side edge of Center Section.
Knit one row, working in the back of each st.
Begin pattern stitch:
Row 1: K 2, yo, k 2 tog, * yo, k 5, yo, sl 1, k 2 tog, psso; rep from * to last 9 sts, yo, k 5, yo, sl 1, k 1, psso, yo, k 2 — 215 sts.
Row 2: K 2, inc in next st, purl to last 3 sts,

inc in next st, k 2 — 217 sts.
Row 3: K 2, yo, k 1, * yo, sl 1, k 2 tog, psso, yo, k 5; rep from * to last 6 sts, yo, sl 1, k 2 tog, psso, yo, k 1, yo, k 2 — 219 sts.
Row 4: K 2, purl to last 2 sts, k 2.
Row 5: K 2, yo, k 2 tog, * yo, k 3, yo, sl 1, k 1, psso, k 1, k 2 tog; rep from * to last 7 sts, yo, k 3, yo, sl 1, k 1, psso, yo, k 2 — 221 sts.
Row 6: Rep Row 2 — 223 sts.
Row 7: K 2, yo, k 1, k 2 tog, * yo, k 1, yo, sl 1, k 2 tog, psso; rep from * to last 6 sts, yo, k 1, yo, sl 1, k 1, psso, k 1, yo, k 2 — 225 sts.
Row 8: Rep Row 4.
Row 9: K 2, * yo, k 5, yo, sl 1, k 2 tog, psso; rep from * to last 7 sts, yo, k 5, yo, k 2 — 227 sts.
Row 10: Rep Row 2 — 229 sts.
Row 11: Rep Row 1 — 231 sts.
Row 12: Rep Row 4.
Row 13: K 2, * yo, k 3, yo, sl 1, k 1, psso, k 1, k 2 tog; rep from * to last 5 sts, yo, k 3, yo, k 2 — 233 sts.
Row 14: Rep Row 2 — 235 sts.
Row 15: K 2, yo, k 2, * yo, sl 1, k 2 tog, psso, yo, k 1; rep from * to last 3 sts, k 1, yo, k 2 — 237 sts.
Row 16: Rep Row 4.
Row 17: K 2, yo, k 3, * yo, sl 1, k 2 tog, psso, yo, k 5; rep from * to last 8 sts, yo, sl 1, k 2 tog, psso, yo, k 3, yo, k 2 — 239 sts.
Row 18: Rep Row 2 — 241 sts.
Row 19: Rep Row 9 — 243 sts.
Row 20: Rep Row 4.
Row 21: K 2, yo, k 1, * yo, sl 1, k 1, psso, k 1, k 2 tog, yo, k 3; rep from * to last 8 sts, yo, sl 1, k 1, psso, k 1, k 2 tog, yo, k 1, yo, k 2 — 245 sts.
Row 22: Rep Row 2 — 247 sts.
Row 23: K 2, yo, k 1, k 2 tog, * yo, k 1, yo, sl 1, k 2 tog, psso; rep from * to last 6 sts,

yo, k 1, yo, sl 1, k 1, psso, k 1, yo, k 2 — 249 sts.

Row 24: Rep Row 4.
Row 25: Rep Row 3 — 251 sts.
Row 26: Rep Row 2 — 253 sts.
Row 27: Rep Row 17 — 255 sts.
Row 28: Rep Row 4.
Row 29: K 2, yo, k 2, * k 2 tog, yo, k 3, yo, sl 1, k 1, psso, k 1; rep from * to last 3 sts, k 1, yo, k 2 — 257 sts.
Row 30: Rep Row 2 — 259 sts.
Row 31: Rep Row 15 — 261 sts.
Row 32: Rep Row 4.
Rep Rows 1 to 32 twice, then Rows 1 to 8 once, dec one st at end of last row — 368 sts.
Continue in Moss Stitch, inc one st at each end of Row 2, then every 4th row until there are 374 sts.
Bind off loosely.

FINISHING

Sew edges of Borders to Center Section. With a slightly damp cloth and warm iron press lightly.

PATCHWORK QUILT

TECHNIQUE: Sewing

MATERIALS

- ☐ 3/8 yard of 45"-wide cream cotton
- ☐ 5/8 yard of 45"-wide lavender cotton
- ☐ 3/4" yard of 45"-wide floral cotton
- ☐ 1 3/4 yards 45"-wide green cotton
- ☐ 34"-49" synthetic batting
- ☐ sewing thread

NOTE: This quilt (about 32" x 47") is composed of four 6-square rows, two borders and a binding which is turned over quiltback. Measure carefully when you cut and stitch 3/8" seams exactly.

DIRECTIONS

1 Quiltblocks: From each of the four fabrics, cut four 2 1/4"-wide strips straight across the fabric width. Using a strip of each color, seam 4 lengths side by side in the order shown (see pincushion). Repeat three times. Cut each length into seven 6 3/4" square quiltblocks. (The extra four blocks can make a pillow or pincushions.)

2 Quilttop: Seam four rows of six quiltblocks, in alternating directions (see photo). Seam the rows side by side. Cut four 2 1/2"-wide lavender borders, two 37" long and two 25" long. Seam longer border at side edges, shorter borders to ends. Cut four 4"-wide floral borders, two 40" long and two 28" long. Seam them the same way.

3 Quilting: Cut a 35" x 50" green quilt-back/binding. Spread it wrong side up. Center batting on top, then the quilttop. Pin, then baste from center outward to each corner and each side. Stitch round each block and the inner border. Trim batting flush with quilt. Trim backing 1" wider, all around, than quilt. Turn the back edges over 1/2" twice and slipstitch the fold to the quilt, to bind it.

DIAPER PIN CUSHION

1 Make two squares as for Patchwork Quilt.

2 Pin squares together with right sides facing each other. Stitch (3/8" seams allowed) around outside edge, leaving small opening for turning. Turn and stuff firmly. Slipstitch opening closed.

Left: Diaper Pin Cushion
Below: Patchwork Quilt

EMBROIDERED NIGHTIE

TECHNIQUE: Sewing

SIZE: 0 to 6 months

MATERIALS

- ☐ 1½ yards of 45"-wide fine cotton voile
- ☐ 3 buttons about 3/16" dia.
- ☐ 2 yards of ruffled lace about 1¼" wide
- ☐ 4 yards of 3/8" lace edging
- ☐ ½ yard of 1/8" elastic
- ☐ ¼ yard of 45"-wide thin interfacing
- ☐ tracing paper
- ☐ sewing thread to match fabric
- ☐ **Optional:** embroidery needle and floss

NOTE: The yoke is faced and there is a center back opening that extends into the skirt. To "cut a pair," pin the pattern to folded fabric. Seam 3/8" deep with the pieces pinned right sides together.

DIRECTIONS

Pattern outline

1 Pattern: Trace the full-size patterns, Nos 1 through 4 (see pullout sheet and the pattern line above).

2 Cutting: With the Center Front (or Center Back) on a fold of doubled fabric, cut 2 each of #3 skirt, #1 front yoke and #2 of back yoke. Cut 1 pair of #4 sleeves. Each back yoke will fold in half at the back opening to make its own facing. At the top of the center fold of the skirt front, cut a small notch to mark the center. On the center fold of the skirt back, cut from the top edge downward to the notch (see pattern).

3 Skirt: Seam 1 edge of each sleeve to the front skirt and the back skirt at the armholes (the concave curves) with zigzag stitch, bind or narrowly hem the slit back edges.

4 Sleeve Edge: Turn under 1/4", then 1/2" and press; stitch this hem. Lap sleeve edge over the straight edge of ruffled lace and edgestitch. Slide 4" of elastic between the 2 rows of stitching and sew down each end.

5 Underarm/Side Seam: Seam front to back at sleeve and side edges, matching armholes and sleeve edges.

6 Yoke: Apply interfacing to wrong side of 1 yoke front and both yoke backs. Seam each yoke back to a yoke front at the shoulder edges. (The yoke backs will overlap each other for the time being.) Starting and ending at the back yoke's "on fold" line, pin ruffled lace edging to the outside curve of the yoke with right sides together and ruffled edge facing the neck. Narrowly hem both ends of the lace and pin it so the stitching line will be 3/8" from the raw edge.

7 Skirt/Sleeves: Sew 2 gathering rows 1/4" apart between the notches at the top edge of the front skirt, of each sleeve, then of each back skirt from a notch to the turned-under edge. Pin skirt to yoke, right sides together over the lace, lining up the CB's and CF's and placing a sleeve seam at each notch. Pull up gathers to fit yoke; stitch. Press seam toward yoke.

8 Yoke Facing: With right sides together, fold each back yoke in half (along with the skirt edge). Pin its shoulder edge to the front yoke facing (which you cut earlier) and press seams open. Seam the facing to the yoke at the neck edge, with shoulder seams matching. Clip the neck's seam allowance. Turn the yoke right side out (along with the skirt facings) and press. Baste raw edges together at each armhole. Turn under the facing's bottom edge and slipstitch it to the yoke seam; press. Topstitch near the yoke, neck and opening edges.

9 Hem: Fold 2½" at the bottom edge, twice; press. Machine stitch the hem and, again, along the fold. Stitch 3/8" lace edging over both rows of stitching.

10 Finishing: Make buttonholes on yoke (see pattern) and sew on buttons.

Optional: Embroider bullion roses on yoke and hem, following the directions opposite.

HOW TO EMBROIDER
BULLION ROSES

Bullion roses are stitched in gradient shades of embroidery floss, starting with darkest shade at center and working out to lightest shade. Stitch leaves in bullion knots (diagram below) or chain stitch in tones of green.

Bring up needle at A. Stitch from B to A; do not pull needle through (A to B equals the width of knot). Twist thread several times around the needle clockwise to equal the width of AB. Pull needle through easing twisted thread onto fabric. Re-insert needle at B. Build up bullion knots as shown below.

A B   A B   A B

EMBROIDERED FACE CLOTH

Make a purchased face cloth very special by embroidering a border of bullion roses as shown, following the instructions above.

Using the same technique, you can add a personal touch to sheets, towels or a simple baby's undershirt.

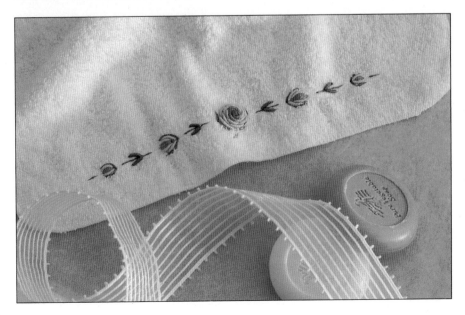

BABY'S BATHTIME

When preparing your baby's bath, make sure that you have everything you will need, such as soap, face cloth and towel, within easy reach. Plan the area around the bath with easy access to storage shelves, changing table and baby's clothes. A nursery basket or box, lined with pretty, washable fabric is ideal for holding all those bits and pieces like powder, diaper pins, baby oil and a pin cushion.

BABY'S DRESS

TECHNIQUE: Knitting and Crocheting

DIRECTIONS
FRONT
Using No. 3 needles, cast on 140 sts.
Work 9 rows in garter st (k every row).
(Row 1 is wrong side).
Work 2 rows in st st (k 1 row, p 1 row).
Beg pattern stitch:
Row 1: K 14, * yo, sl 1, k 1, psso, k 20; rep from * ending last rep with k 14, instead of k 20.
Row 2 and All Even Numbered Rows: Purl.
Row 3: K 12, * k 2 tog, yo, k 1, yo, sl 1, k 1, psso, k 17; rep from * ending last rep with k 13, instead of k 17.
Row 5: K 11, * k 2 tog, yo, sl 1, k 2 tog, psso, yo, sl 1, k 1, psso, k 15; rep from * ending last rep with k 12, instead of k 15.
Row 7: K 13, * yo, k 1, yo, k 19; rep from * ending last rep with k 14, instead of k 19.
Row 9: K 25, * yo, sl 1, k 1, psso, k 20; rep from * ending last rep with k 25, instead of k 20.
Row 11: K 23, * k 2 tog, yo, k 1, yo, sl 1, k 1, psso, k 17; rep from * ending last rep with k 24, instead of k 17.
Row 13: K 22, * k 2 tog, yo, sl 1, k 2 tog, psso, yo, sl 1, k 1, psso, k 15; rep from * ending last rep with k 23, instead of k 15.
Row 15: K 24, * yo, k 1, yo, k 19; rep from * ending last rep with k 25, instead of k 19.
Row 17: K 25, * yo, k 2 tog, k 20; rep from * ending last rep with k 25, instead of k 20.

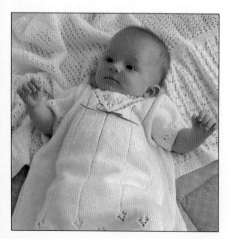

SIZE
Directions are given for size 6 months.

MATERIALS
Fingering-Weight Yarn (50 gr. ball): 4 balls; 1 pair each of No. 1 and No. 3 knitting needles, *or any size needles to obtain the gauge below;* Size C crochet hook; 3 buttons.

GAUGE
On No. 3 needles in stockinette stitch (st st) — 8 sts = 1"; 11 rows = 1". Be sure to check your gauge.

MEASUREMENTS
Size (mos.):   6
Body Chest: 18"
Finished Measurements:
Chest: 19 1/4"
Length to Back Neck: 18 3/4"
Sleeve Length: 2"

Row 18: Purl.
Rep Rows 17 and 18 until work measures 6" from beg, ending with a purl row.
Dec row: K 12, k 2 tog, k 11, * yo, k 2 tog, k 9, k 2 tog, k 9; rep from * until 27 sts rem, yo, k 2 tog, k 11, k 2 tog, k 12 — 134 sts.
Next Row: Purl.
Next Row: K 24, * yo, k 2 tog, k 19; rep from * ending with k 24, instead of k 19.
Next Row: Purl.
Rep last 2 rows until work measures 7" from beg, ending with a purl row.
Dec row: K 11, k 2 tog, k 11, * yo, k 2 tog, k 8, k 2 tog, k 9; rep from * until 26 sts rem, yo, k 2 tog, k 11, k 2 tog, k 11 — 128 sts.
Next Row: Purl.
Next Row: K 23, * yo, k 2 tog, k 18; rep from * ending last rep with k 23, instead of k 18.
Next Row: Purl.
Rep last 2 rows until work measures 8" from beg, ending with a purl row.
Dec row: K 10, k 2 tog, k 11, * yo, k 2 tog, k 8, k 2 tog, k 8; rep from * until 25 sts rem, yo, k 2 tog, k 10, k 2 tog, k 11 — 122 sts.
Next Row: Purl.
Next Row: K 22, * yo, k 2 tog, k 17; rep from * ending last rep with k 22, instead of k 17.

Next Row: Purl.
Rep last 2 rows until work measures 9" from beg, ending with a purl row.
Dec row: K 10, k 2 tog, k 10, * yo, k 2 tog, k 7, k 2 tog, k 8; rep from * until 24 sts rem, yo, k 2 tog, k 10, k 2 tog, k 10 — 116 sts.
Next Row: Purl.
Next Row: K 21, * yo, k 2 tog, k 16; rep from * until 21 sts rem, yo, k 2 tog, k 19.
Next Row: Purl.
Rep last 2 rows until work measures 10" from beg, ending with a purl row.
Dec row: K 8, k 2 tog, k 1, k 2 tog, k 8, * yo, k 2 tog, k 5, k 2 tog, k 1, k 2 tog, k 6; rep from * until 23 sts rem, yo, k 2 tog, k 8, k 2 tog, k 1, k 2 tog, k 8 — 104 sts.
Next Row: Purl.
Next Row: K 19, * yo, k 2 tog, k 14; rep from * ending last rep with k 19, instead of k 14.
Next Row: Purl.
Rep last 2 rows until work measures 11" from beg, ending with a purl row.
Dec row: K 7, k 2 tog, k 1, k 2 tog, k 7, * yo, k 2 tog, k 4, k 2 tog, k 1, k 2 tog, k 5; rep from * until 21 sts rem, yo, k 2 tog, k 7, k 2 tog, k 1, k 2 tog, k 7 — 92 sts.
Next Row: Purl. **
Beg Yoke:
Row 1: K 17, yo, k 2 tog, k 12, yo, k 2 tog, k 10, k 2 tog, yo, k 1, yo, sl 1, k 1, psso, k 11, yo, k 2 tog, k 12, yo, k 2 tog, k 17.
Row 2 and All Even Numbered Rows: Purl.
Row 3: K 17, yo, k 2 tog, k 12, yo, k 2 tog, k 9, k 2 tog, yo, k 3, yo, sl 1, k 1, psso, k 10, yo, k 2 tog, k 12, yo, k 2 tog, k 17.
Row 5: K 17, yo, k 2 tog, k 12, yo, k 2 tog, k 8, k 2 tog, yo, k 5, yo, sl 1, k 1, psso, k 9, yo, k 2 tog, k 12, yo, k 2 tog, k 17.
Row 7: K 6, k 2 tog, k 1, k 2 tog, k 6, yo, k 2 tog, k 3, k 2 tog, k 1, k 2 tog, k 4, yo, k 2 tog, k 3, k 2 tog, k 2, k 2 tog, yo, k 3, yo, sl 1, k 1, psso, k 2, yo, sl 1, k 1, psso k 3, k 2 tog, k 3, yo, k 2 tog, k 4, k 2 tog, k 1, k 2 tog, k 3, yo, k 2 tog, k 7, k 2 tog, k 1, k 2 tog, k 5 — 82 sts.
Row 9: K 15, yo, k 2 tog, k 10, yo, k 2 tog, k 5, k 2 tog, yo, k 2, k 2 tog, yo, k 1, yo, sl 1, k 1, psso, k 2, yo, sl 1, k 1, psso, k 6, yo, k 2 tog, k 10, yo, k 2 tog, k 15 — 82 sts.
Row 11: K 15, yo, k 2 tog, k 10, yo, k 2 tog, k 4, k 2 tog, yo, k 2, k 2 tog, yo, sl 1, k 2 tog, psso, yo, sl 1, k 1, psso, k 2, yo, sl 1, k 1, psso, k 5, yo, k 2 tog, k 10, yo, k 2 tog, k 15 — 80 sts.
Row 13: K 15, yo, k 2 tog, k 10, yo, k 2 tog, k 3, k 2 tog, yo, k 5, yo, k 1, yo, k 5, yo, sl 1, k 1, psso, k 4, yo, k 2 tog, k 10, yo, k 2

tog, k 15 — 82 sts.

Row 14: Purl.

Armhole Shaping:

Row 15: Bind off 3 sts, k 3 (this includes st left on right-hand needle from bind-off), (k 2 tog) twice, k 5, yo, k 2 tog, k 3, (k 2 tog) twice, k 3, yo, k 2 tog, k 2, k 2 tog, yo, k 3, yo, sl 1, k 1, psso, k 6, yo, sl 1, k 1, psso, k 2, yo, sl 1, k 1, psso, k 3, yo, k 2 tog, k 3, (k 2 tog) twice, k 3, yo, k 2 tog, k 5, (k 2 tog) twice, k 6 — 71 sts.

Row 16: Bind off 3 sts, purl to end — 68 sts.

Row 17: K 2 tog, (k 8, yo, k 2 tog) twice, k 1, k 2 tog, yo, k 2, k 2 tog, yo, k 1, yo, sl 1, k 1, psso, k 3, k 2 tog, yo, k 1, yo, sl 1, k 1, psso, k 2, yo, sl 1, k 1, psso, k 2, (yo, k 2 tog, k 8) twice, k 2 tog.

Row 18: P 2 tog, purl to last 2 sts, p 2 tog.

Row 19: K 2 tog, k 6, yo, k 2 tog, k 8, yo, (k 2 tog) twice, yo, k 2, k 2 tog, yo, sl 1, k 2 tog, psso, yo, sl 1, k 1, psso, k 1, k 2 tog, yo, sl 1, k 2 tog, psso, yo, sl 1, k 1, psso, k 2, yo, sl 1, k 1, psso, k 1, yo, k 2 tog, k 8, yo, k 2 tog, k 6, k 2 tog.

Row 20: P 2 tog, purl to last 2 sts, p 2 tog — 60 sts.

Row 21: K 6, yo, k 2 tog, k 8, yo, k 3 tog, yo, (k 5, yo, k 1, yo) twice, k 5, yo, sl 1, k 1, psso, yo, k 2 tog, k 8, yo, k 2 tog, k 6.

Row 22 and All Even Numbered Rows: Purl.

Row 23: K 6, yo, k 2 tog, k 8, k 2 tog, yo, k 3, yo, sl 1, k 1, psso, k 14, yo, sl 1, k 1, psso, k 2, yo, sl 1, k 1, psso, k 9, yo, k 2 tog, k 6.

Row 25: K 6, yo, k 2 tog, k 7, k 2 tog, yo, k 2, k 2 tog, yo, k 1, yo, sl 1, k 1, psso, k 11, k 2 tog, yo, k 1, yo, sl 1, k 1, psso, k 2, yo, sl 1, k 1, psso, k 8, yo, k 2 tog, k 6.

Row 27: K 6, yo, k 2 tog, k 6, k 2 tog, yo, k 2, k 2 tog, yo, sl 1, k 2 tog, psso, yo, sl 1, k 1, psso, k 9, k 2 tog, yo, sl 1, k 2 tog, psso, yo, sl 1, k 1, psso, k 2, yo, sl 1, k 1, psso, k 7, yo, k 2 tog, k 6.

Row 29: K 6, yo, k 2 tog, k 5, k 2 tog, yo, k 5, yo, k 1, yo, k 13, yo, k 1, yo, k 5, yo, sl 1, k 1, psso, k 6, yo, k 2 tog, k 6.

Keeping in pat, work 7 rows more.

Neck Shaping:

Row 37: K 6, yo, k 2 tog, k 1, k 2 tog, yo, k 5, yo, k 1, yo, k 3, bind off next 16 sts, k 2 (this includes st left on right-hand needle from bind-off), yo, k 1, yo, k 5, yo, sl 1, k 1, psso, k 2, yo, k 2 tog, k 6 — 44 sts.

Keeping in pat, continue on last 22 sts, dec one st at neck edge in every row 4 times — 18 sts.

Row 42: Purl.

Row 43: K 2 tog, yo, sl 1, k 2 tog, psso, yo, sl 1, k 1, psso, k 2, yo, sl 1, k 1, psso, k 7.

Keeping in pat, work 6 rows more.

Bind off.

Join yarn at neck edge and complete other side of neck to correspond with first side.

BACK

Work as for Front to **

Next Row: K 17, * yo, k 2 tog, k 12; rep from * until 19 sts rem, yo, k 2 tog, k 17.

Next Row: Purl.

Rep last 2 rows twice.

Dec row: K 6, k 2 tog, k 1, k 2 tog, k 6, yo, k 2 tog, k 3, k 2 tog, k 1, k 2 tog, k 4, yo, k 2 tog, (k 5, k 2 tog, k 5, yo, k 2 tog) twice, k 3, k 2 tog, k 1, k 2 tog, k 4, yo, k 2 tog, k 6, k 2 tog, k 1, k 2 tog, k 6 — 82 sts.

Next Row: Purl.

Next Row: K 15, yo, k 2 tog, k 10, yo, k 2 tog, (k 11, yo, k 2 tog twice), k 10, yo, k 2 tog, k 15.

Next Row: Purl.

Divide for Back Opening:

Next Row: K 15, yo, k 2 tog, k 10, yo, k 2 tog, k 9, turn, cast on 6 sts. Continue on last 44 sts.

Next Row: K 6, purl to end.

Next Row: K 15, yo, k 2 tog, k 10, yo, k 2 tog, k 15.

Next Row: K 6, purl to end.

Armhole Shaping:

Next Row: Bind off 3 sts, k 3 (this includes st left on right-hand needle from bind-off), (k 2 tog) twice, k 5, yo, k 2 tog, k 3, (k 2 tog) twice, k 3, yo, k 2 tog, k 15 — 37 sts.

Next Row: K 6, purl to end.

Next Row: K 2 tog, k 8, yo, k 2 tog, k 8, yo, k 2 tog, k 15.

Next Row: K 6, purl to last 2 sts, p 2 tog — 35 sts.
Next Row: K 2 tog, k 6, yo, k 2 tog, k 8, yo, k 2 tog, k 15.
Next Row: K 6, purl to last 2 sts, p 2 tog — 33 sts.
Keeping in pat, continue until there are 3 rows less than Front to Shoulder Shaping.
Back Neck Shaping:
Keeping in pat, bind off 13 sts, purl to end. Dec one st at neck edge in every row twice — 18 sts.
Bind off.
Join yarn to rem sts and continue as follows:
Next Row: K 15, yo, k 2 tog, k 10, yo, k 2 tog, k 15.
Next Row: Purl to last 6 sts, k 6.
Next Row: K 3, yo, k 2 tog (buttonhole), k 10, yo, k 2 tog, k 10, yo, k 2 tog, k 15.
Next Row: Purl to last 6 sts, k 6.
Next Row: K 15, yo, k 2 tog, k 3, (k 2 tog) twice, k 3, yo, k 2 tog, k 5, (k 2 tog) twice, k 6.
Work to correspond with other side, working 2 more buttonholes as before evenly

along back opening and begin armhole shaping on next row as before.
SLEEVES
Using No. 1 needles, cast on 42 sts.
Work 7 rows in garter st (Row 1 is wrong side).
Change to No. 3 needles.
Next Row: K 2, * knit into next st, twice, k 1; rep from * to end — 62 sts.
Next Row: Purl.
Beg pattern:
Row 1: K 5, * yo, sl 1, k 1, psso, k 8; rep from * ending last rep with k 5, instead of k 8.
Row 2 and All Even Numbered Rows: Purl.
Row 3: K 3, * k 2 tog, yo, k 1, yo, sl 1, k 1, psso, k 5; rep from * ending last rep with k 4, instead of k 5.
Row 5: K 2, * k 2 tog, yo, sl 1, k 2 tog, psso, yo, sl 1, k 1, psso, k 3; rep from * to end.
Row 7: K 4, * yo, k 1, yo, k 7; rep from * ending last rep with k 5, instead of k 7.
Row 8: Purl.
Continue in st st until work measures 2" from beg, ending with a purl row.

Cap Shaping:
Dec one st at each end of every row until 18 sts rem.
Bind off.

FINISHING

Sew shoulder, side and sleeve seams. Sew in sleeves, easing extra fullness across top of sleeve. Sew the 6 cast-on sts at back opening in place. Using Size C crochet hook, work one row of sc evenly around neck edge, having a number divisible by three plus one.
Next round: Ch 1, * sc into each of next sc, ch 3, slip st back into first ch from hook; rep from * to last sc, sc in last sc. Fasten off. Sew on buttons.

FLORAL BUNNY

TECHNIQUE: Sewing

Make this nursery charmer following the directions for the bunny on page 15.

♥ **HINT** ♥

Trims and fabric should always be of the same material to avoid problems when washing and ironing. A synthetic trim on a cotton sheet may well melt under a hot iron while an iron on a cooler setting won't press out wrinkles from cotton. Keep this in mind when choosing ribbons, binding, appliqués and lace.

EYELET LACE SHEETS

TECHNIQUE : Sewing

MATERIALS
☐ 60" of 45"-wide eyelet cotton
☐ 47" long eyelet lace
☐ 1⅝ yards of ⅜"-wide satin ribbon.

DIRECTIONS
1 Sew eyelet lace to top edge of eyelet cotton fabric. Finish raw edges as desired. Stitch ribbon over seam, and tie into a bow at center.
2 Hem all raw edges of sheet.

NURSERY BASICS

Your baby's nursery will be a special place for the two of you to share. With a little imagination, some planning and not a great deal of money, you can turn a small room or even a quiet corner into a pretty haven. Here are some basic elements you will need to provide:

☐ **Bassinet** or **crib**
New babies sleep best in a reasonably confined, cozy space, but soon outgrow this. You will have to make your own decision as to when your baby moves to a crib. The most important feature to look for when choosing a crib is safety. The sides should be securely held in place by child-proof latches. The bars should be close together so that your baby can't get stuck between them. The mattress should be firm and fit in the crib securely so that a little head and fingers can't be trapped beneath. Some bedtime extras you will need are: a plastic mattress protector; a fitted bottom sheet; mosquito net; crib bumper and a colorful mobile or toy to suspend over the crib.

☐ **Changing table**
Any firm horizontal surface, such as a table top, old desk or chest of drawers, can become a very useful changing table. Cover the surface with a washable or wipeable covering. For very small babies a foam pad with raised sides can be a secure cradle when changing or dressing baby. Ideally the changing table will have some drawers for holding all those change time essentials, such as creams, powder, pins, tissues, washcloth and even a favorite toy to amuse baby at changing time.

☐ **Storage**
You will be amazed at how much "stuff" such a little person needs. Plan for storage of various kinds to be nearest the place where the items will be used. Open shelves above the changing table are ideal for stacking clean diapers, while drawers and cupboards are best for clothes. Some form of toy storage — stackable plastic cubes, shelves or a basket — will also be useful.

☐ **Chair**
Place a comfortable chair or rocker, preferably with arm rests, in a quiet corner for feeding baby or simply a moment's rest.

☐ **Diaper Pail**
A simple plastic covered pail is fine for soaking soiled diapers. If you plan to use disposable diapers they can be tossed in the pail.

☐ **Bath**
Like the bassinet, small plastic babies' baths are best for the newborn. You will know when it's time to move to the family bath tub. Make sure that you have all of baby's bathtime needs at hand before you begin.

☐ **Night light**
You are sure to be making many middle-of-the-night visits to the nursery. A night light, or dimmer switch on the main light, will allow you to move around comfortably without disturbing the baby.

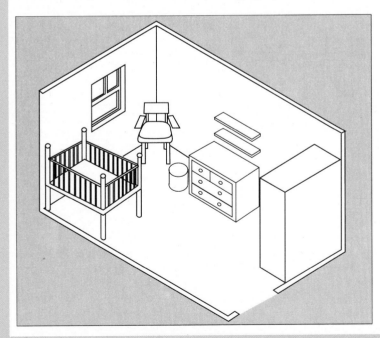

Blossom

The promise of beautiful things to come – babies and blossoms just seem to go together. Even the huge, cuddly bunny is decked out in the prettiest floral print. If you've always wanted to try smocking, this little dress is the perfect way to begin. Remember to make the shoes and pants to complete the picture and top it all off with a warm, textured cardigan.

SMOCKED DRESS AND PANTIES

TECHNIQUE: Sewing

SIZE: 6 to 12 months

MATERIALS

- ☐ 1⁷/₈ yards of 45"-wide lightweight cotton
- ☐ 3 buttons about ³/₈" dia.
- ☐ 2¹/₄ yards of ruffled lace edging
- ☐ elastic – 1¹/₂ yards of ¹/₈"-wide and ³/₄ yard of ¹/₄"-wide
- ☐ embroidery floss and needle
- ☐ tracing paper
- ☐ sewing threads (to match and to contrast)

NOTE: The yoke is faced and there is a center back opening that extends into the skirt. To "cut a pair," pin the pattern to folded fabric. Seam ³/₈" deep with the pieces pinned right sides together.

DIRECTIONS

Pattern outline 〰〰〰〰〰〰〰

1 Cutting: Follow Steps 1 and 2 of Yellow Dotted Dress on page 22 but omit the ruffles.

2 Yoke: Seam each yoke back to a yoke front at the shoulder edges. (The yoke backs will overlap each other for the time being.)

3 Back Skirt: Follow Step 5 of Yellow Dotted Dress. Sew a gathering row at each top edge from the notch to the Center Back line (see pattern).

4 Front Skirt: On the wrong side between the 2 notches (see pattern), transfer the smocking dots (see Step 1, opposite) with the first row ¹/₄" from the top edge. Pull up the threads (Step 3, opposite) to 8" wide. Start to smock at the second row with an outline stitch. Then make up your own smocked border. We went on to a row of honeycomb, a row of outline, 2 rows of surface honeycomb, a row of outline and 3 rows of wave stitches. Bullion knots and daisy stitches are spaced between the waves.

5 Assembly: With right sides together, pin skirts to yoke with notches matching, side edges even and the Center Backs (see pattern) lined up. Pull up back gathers to fit yoke. Stitch.

6 Yoke Facing: With right sides together, fold each back yoke in half (along with the skirt facings). Pin its shoulder edge to the front yoke facing; stitch and press seams open. Seam the neck edge, with shoulder seams matching. Turn the yoke right side out (along with the skirt edge) and press the folded back edges. Baste raw edges together at each armhole. Turn under the facing's bottom edge and slipstitch it to the yoke seam.

7 Sleeves: Gather top edge of each sleeve between notches. Pin sleeves to

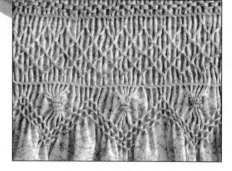

dress at armhole edges. Draw up gathers to fit; stitch. At the wrist edge, turn under 1³/₄" and press. Turn under the raw edge and stitch a 1¹/₂" hem. Stitch again ¹/₄" away to make the casing. Lap the wrist edge over the ruffled lace and topstitch. Insert 6"-long elastic through the casing and stitch across each end.

8 Underarm Side Seam: Seam front dress to back at each sleeve and side edge, matching armholes and edges.

9 Lower Edge: Hem the dress. Lap the hem over ruffled lace and topstitch, turning under raw ends.

10 Back Opening: Make buttonholes and sew on buttons.

11 Panties: Follow Step 13 of Yellow Dotted Dress on page 22.

SIMPLE SMOCKING

Smocking began as the first "elastic" but has become a delightful and creative technique for trimming babies' and children's clothes.

Follow these illustrated steps to master the technique and some of the most common smocking stitches.

PREPARE YOUR FABRIC

STEP 1 Mark a grid of dots on wrong side of fabric by using graph paper as a guide. Place dressmaker's carbon paper under the fabric, and pinning graph paper on top, firmly mark dots.

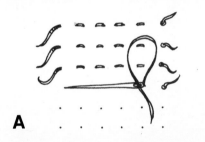

A

STEP 2 Gathering up dots: With strong, doubled thread in a contrasting color, begin at right hand side and pick up each dot across fabric. Leave thread hanging at end of each row. (Fig. A).

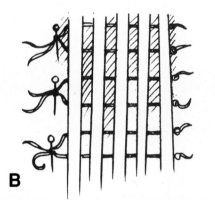

B

STEP 3 Pulling up: Pull up threads until fabric is desired width, for example width of yoke. (Fig. B). Tie off threads firmly in pairs. Pull up firmly, but not tightly. Secure threads. Begin smocking on right side of the fabric. Remove gathering threads when smocking is complete.

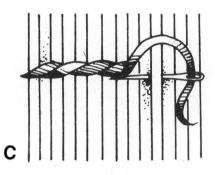

C

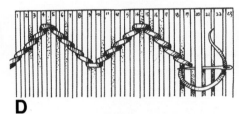

D

E

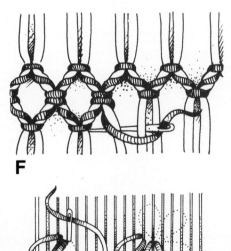

F

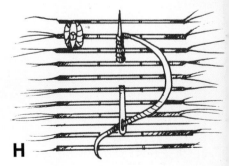

G

H

OUTLINE STITCH (Fig. C): Work stitch with thread above needle as shown and keeping stitches tight.

WAVE STITCH (Fig. D): Work stitches firmly although angles make this stitch very elastic. Always work between two rows of gathering stitches, beginning at lower left corner and working up as shown. When ascending, thread lies above the needle and below the needle when descending.

HONEYCOMBING (Fig. E): One of the oldest smocking stitches, it is very elastic and simple to do. Stagger starting points of stitches, working over two folds.

SURFACE HONEYCOMB (Fig. F): This stitch is elastic and very decorative, exposing more thread. It can be built up into panels by mirror reversing the panels.

LAZY DAISY STITCH (Fig. G) and **BULLION KNOTS** (Fig. H): These are worked as if embroidering but take care to begin and end stitches on folds as shown.

SHOES

TECHNIQUE: Sewing

SIZE: 6 to 12 months

MATERIALS
- ☐ 8" x 20" each of outer fabric and lining
- ☐ 8" x 20" of iron-on interfacing
- ☐ 2 buttons ¹/₂" or smaller
- ☐ tracing paper

Note: With right sides facing, seam ¹/₄" from the raw edges. Clip the seam allowance at curves.

DIRECTIONS

1 Cutting: Trace the two full-size patterns below. Placing its center back on a fold of fabric, cut two uppers each from the outer fabric, lining and interfacing. Cut two soles from the same three fabrics.

2 Interfacing: Iron the interfacing to the wrong side of the outer pieces.

3 Seaming: Sew the center front seam (A to B) of each upper. Press it open. Turn it right side out and topstitch at each side of the seam. Seam a sole to each upper, matching centers at B and C. Press open, turn and topstitch.

4 Lining: Repeat Step 3 with lining pieces. With right sides together, pin the lining over the shoe, matched at CB and CF and edges even. Stitch the raw edges, leaving a back opening for turning. Trim seams, turn and edgestitch.

5 Buttons: Make buttonholes and sew on the buttons.

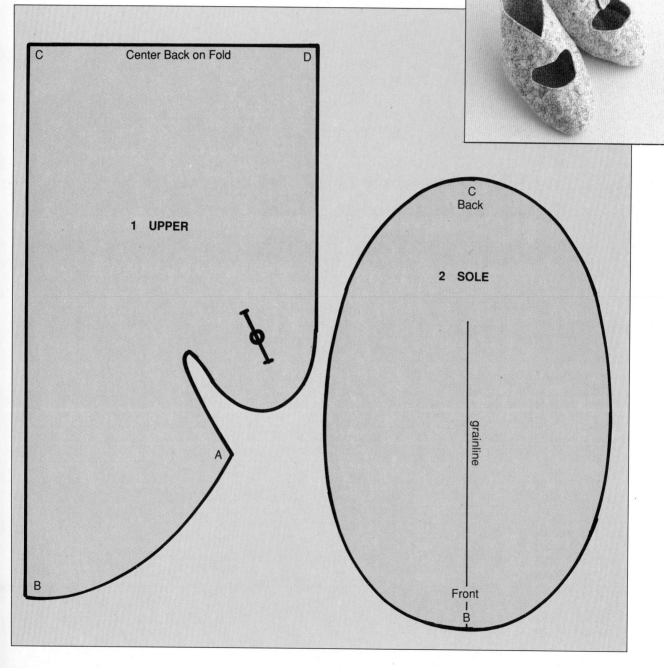

CARDIGAN WITH BOWS

TECHNIQUE: Knitting

DIRECTIONS
BACK
Using No. 1 needles and A, cast on 75(83,91,99) sts.
Row 1: K 2, * p 1, k 1, rep from * to last st, k 1.
Row 2: K 1, * p 1, k 1, rep from * to end.
Rep Rows 1 and 2 once.
Row 5: Using Mc, knit.
Row 6: Rep Row 2.
Rep Rows 1 and 2 twice.
Using A, rep Rows 5 and 6 once.
Rep Rows 1 and 2 once.
Change to No. 3 needles and Mc .**
Work in st st (k 1 row, p 1 row) until work measures 5(6,7,8½)" from beg, ending with a purl row.
Armhole Shaping:
Bind off 5(5,6,6) sts at beg of next 2 rows.
Dec one st at each end every other row until 57(63,69,75) sts rem.
Work 33(35,39,41) rows.
Shoulder Shaping:
Bind off 8(9,10,11) sts at beg of next 2 rows, then 8(10,11,12) sts at beg of next 2 rows.
Bind off rem 25(25,27,29) sts for back neck.
LEFT FRONT
Using No. 1 needles and A, cast on 37(41,45,49) sts.
Work as given for Back to **.
Row 1: K 6(7,8,9), [yo, k 2 tog, k 9(10,11,12)] twice, yo, k 2 tog, k 7(8,9,10).
Row 2: Purl.
Rep last 2 rows 6(8,12,14) times more, then Rows 1 and 2 once.
Next Row: K 17(19,21,23), yo, k 2 tog, k 18(20,22,24).
Next Row: Purl.
Rep last 2 rows 4(6,6,8) times more.
Continue in st st until work measures same as Back to underarm, ending with a purl row.
Armhole and Front Neck Shaping:
Bind off 5(5,6,6) sts at beg of next row.
Dec one st at armhole edge every other row 4(5,5,6) times, **at the same time** dec one st at front edge every other row 5(3,3,3)

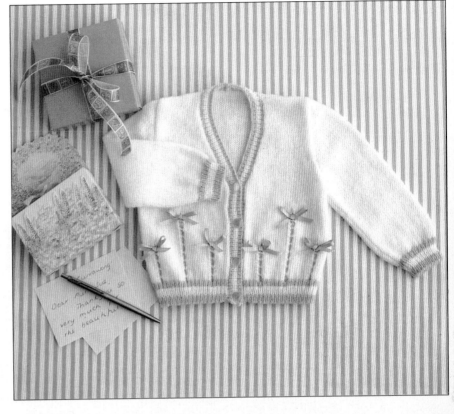

SIZE
Directions are given for size 3 months. Changes for 6 months, 9 months and 12 months are in parentheses.

MATERIALS
Fingering-Weight yarn (50 gr. ball): 3(3,4,4) balls main color (Mc), 1 ball contrasting color (A); 1 pair each No. 1 and No. 3 knitting needles, *or any size needles to obtain gauge below;* 4(4,5,5) small buttons; ribbon.

GAUGE
On No. 3 needles in stockinette stitch (st st) — 8 sts = 1"; 11 rows = 1". Be sure to check your gauge.

MEASUREMENTS
Sizes (mos.):	3	6	9	12
Body Chest:	16"	18"	20"	22"
Finished Measurements:				
Chest:	18"	20"	22"	24"
Length to Back Neck:				
	9"	10"	12"	13½"
Sleeve Length:				
	5½"	6½"	8"	9½"

times, then every 4th row until 16(19,21,23) sts rem.
Work even for 3 rows.
Shoulder Shaping:
Bind off 8(9,10,11) sts at beg of next row.
Work even for 1 row.
Bind off.
RIGHT FRONT
Work Right Front to correspond with Left Front, reversing shaping and working one row more before armhole and shoulder shaping.
SLEEVES
Using No. 1 needles and A, cast on 41(43,45,45) sts.
Work 14 rows in rib and stripes as given for Back, inc 8 sts evenly across last row — 49(51,53,53) sts.
Change to No. 3 needles and Mc.
Continue in st st inc one st at each end of 5th row, then every 8th(10th,10th,12th) row until there are 57(55,59,63) sts, **2nd, 3rd and 4th sizes only** — then every (12th,12th,14th) row until there are (59,63,65) sts.
Work even until length measures 5½ (6½,8,9½)" from beg, ending with a purl row.
Cap Shaping:
Bind off 2(2,3,3) sts at beg of next 2 rows.
Dec one st at each end of next and every

other row until 33(33,29,29) sts rem, then every row until 11 sts rem. Bind off.

RIGHT FRONT BAND
Sew shoulder seams. With right side facing, using No. 1 needles and A, pick up and k 109(121,139,157) sts evenly along right front edge to center of back neck.

Row 1: K 1, * p 1, k 1, rep from * to end

Row 2: Using Mc, knit.

Row 3: Rep Row 1.

Row 4: Rib 4, [yo, k 2 tog, rib 15(17,15,17)] 3(3,4,4) times, yo, k 2 tog, rib to end — *4(4,5,5) buttonholes made.*

Row 5: Rep Row 1.

Row 6: Using A, rep Row 2.

Row 7: Rep Row 1.

Bind off loosely in rib.

LEFT FRONT BAND
Using No. 1 needles and A, beg at center of back neck, pick up and k 109(121,139,157) sts evenly along half of back neck and along left front edge. Complete as for Right Front Band omitting buttonholes.

FINISHING
Press lightly on wrong side with cool iron. Sew side and sleeve seams, sew bands together at center back neck. Sew in sleeves. Sew on buttons. Thread ribbon through eyelet holes on Fronts. Make 6 small bows and attach to top of ribbon on each Front as shown. Sew on buttons.

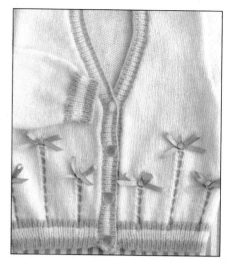

CABLE CARDIGAN

TECHNIQUE: Knitting

DIRECTIONS
BACK
Using No. 1 needles, cast on 75(83,91,99) sts.

Row 1: K 2, * p 1, k 1, rep from * to last st, k 1.

Row 2: K 1, * p 1, k 1, rep from * to end.
Rep Rows 1 and 2, 12 times more, inc 12(14,16,16) sts evenly across last row — 87(97,107,115) sts.
Change to No. 3 needles.
Begin pat:
Row 1: P 1(6,0,1), k 1(1,0,1), p 3(3,1,3), * k 6, p 4, k 1, p 3, rep from * to last 12(17,8,12) sts, k 6, p 4(4,2,4), k 1(1,0,1), p 1(6,0,1).

Row 2 and All Even Numbered Rows: Knit all knit sts and purl all purl sts as they face you.
Rep Rows 1 and 2 twice more.

Row 7: P 1(6,0,1), k 1(1,0,1), p 3(3,1,3), * C6F, p 4, k 1, p 3, rep from * to last 12(17,8,12) sts, C6F, p 4(4,2,4), k 1(1,0,1), p 1(6,0,1).

Row 8: Rep Row 2.

Rows 9-12: Rep Rows 1 and 2 twice more.

Row 13: P 8(3,4,8), k 1(0,1,1), p 3(0,3,3), * k 6, p 4, k 1, p 3, rep from * to last 5(10,1,5) sts, k 0(6,0,0), p 5(4,1,5).

Row 14: Rep Row 2.
Rep Rows 13 and 14 twice more.

Row 19: P 8(3,4,8), k 1(0,1,1), p 3(0,3,3),

SIZE
Directions are given for size 3 months. Changes for 6 months, 9 months and 12 months are in parentheses.

MATERIALS
Fingering-Weight yarn (50 gr. ball): 2(3,3,4) balls; 1 pair each No. 1 and No. 3 knitting needles, *or any size needles to obtain gauge below*; 2 stitch holders; 6(6,6,7) buttons; one cable needle; tapestry needle.

GAUGE
On No. 3 needles in stockinette stitch (st st) — 8 sts = 1"; 11 rows = 1". On No. 3 needles in cable pattern — 19 sts = 2"; 11 rows = 1". Be sure to check your gauge.

MEASUREMENTS
Sizes (mos.):	3	6	9	12
Body Chest:	16"	18"	20"	22"
Finished Measurements:				
Chest:	18"	20"	22"	24"
Length to Back Neck:				
		9"	10"	12"	13½"
Sleeve Length:				
		5"	6"	7"	8"

STITCHES
C6F: Slip next 3 sts onto a cable needle and hold in front of work, K 3, then k 3 from cable needle.

---

* C6F, p 4, k 1, p 3, rep from * to last 5(10,1,5) sts, (C6F) 0(1,0,0) times, p 5(4,1,5).

Row 20: Rep Row 2.

Rep Rows 13 and 14 twice more.
Rep last 24 rows for cable pattern.
Continue in pat until work measures 9(10,12,13)" from beg, working last row on wrong side.

Shoulder Shaping:
Keeping in pat , bind off 10(11,13,14) sts at beg of next 4 rows, then 10(12,12,13) sts at beg of next 2 rows.
Leave rem 27(29,31,33) sts on a stitch holder for back neck.

LEFT FRONT
Using No. 1 needles, cast on 37(41,45,49) sts.
Work 26 rows in rib as given for lower band of Back, inc 6(7,8,8) sts evenly across last row — 43(48,53,57) sts.
Change to No. 3 needles. **
Row 1: P 1(6,0,1), k 1(1,0,1), p 3(3,1,3), (k 6, p 4, k 1, p 3) 2(2,3,3) times, k 6, p 4.

Row 2 and All Even Numbered Rows: Knit all knit sts and purl all purl sts as they face you.
Rep Rows 1 and 2 twice more.

Row 7: P 1(6,0,1), k 1(1,0,1), p 3(3,1,3), (C6F, p 4, k 1, p 3) 2(2,3,3) times, C6F, p 4.

Row 8: Rep Row 2.

Rows 9-12: Rep Rows 1 and 2 twice more.

Row 13: P 8(3,4,8), k 1(0,1,1), p 3(0,3,3,), (k 6, p 4, k 1, p 3) 2(3,3,3) times, p 3.

Row 14: Rep Row 2.

Rows 15-18: Rep Rows 13 and 14 twice more.

Row 19: P 8(3,4,8), k 1(0,1,1), p 3(0,3,3), (C6F, p 4, k 1, p 3) 2(3,3,3) times, p 3.

Row 20: Rep Row 2.

Rows 21-24: Rep Rows 13 and 14 twice more.

Rep last 24 rows for cable pat.
Continue in pat until there are 17(19,21,23)

rows less than Back to Shoulder shaping.

Neck Shaping:

Next Row (wrong side): Bind off 7(8,9,10) sts, work in pat to end.

Work even for 1 row.

Keeping in pat, dec one st at neck edge every other row 6 times — 30(34,38,41) sts.

Work even for 3(5,7,9) rows in pat.

Shoulder Shaping:

Bind off 10(11,13,14) sts at beg of next row and every other row once.

Work even for 1 row.

Bind off.

RIGHT FRONT

Work as for Left Front to **.

Row 1: P 3, (k 6, p 4, k 1, p 3) 2(2,3,3) times, k 6, p 4(4,2,4), k 1(1,0,1), p 1(6,0,1).

Row 2 and All Even Numbered Rows: Knit all knit sts and purl all purl sts as they face you.

Rep Rows 1 and 2 twice more.

Row 7: P 3, (C6F, p 4, k 1, p 3) 2(2,3,3) times, C6F, p 4(4,2,4), k 1(1,0,1), p 1(6,0,1).

Row 8: Rep Row 2.

Rows 9-12: Rep Rows 1 and 2 twice more.

Row 13: P 6, k 1, p 3, (k 6, p 4, k 1, p 3) 2(2,3,3) times, k 0(6,0,0), p 5(4,1,5).

Row 14: Rep Row 2.

Rows 15-18: Rep Rows 13 and 14 twice more.

Row 19: P 6, k 1, p 3, (C6F, p 4, k 1, p 3) 2(2,3,3) times, (C6F) 0(1,0,0) times, p 5(4,1,5).

Row 20: Rep Row 2.

Rows 21-24: Rep Rows 13 and 14 twice more.

Rep last 24 rows for cable pattern.

Continue in pat until there are 16(18,20,22) rows less than Back to shoulder shaping.

Neck Shaping:

Next Row (right side): Bind off 7(8,9,10) sts, work in pat to end.

Keeping in pat , dec one st at neck edge every other row 6 times — 30(34,38,41) sts.

Work even for 4(6,8,10) rows in pat.

Shoulder Shaping:

Complete as for Left Front.

SLEEVES

Using No. 1 needles, cast on 43(47,49,49) sts.

Work 26 rows in rib as given for lower band of Back, inc 10 sts evenly across last row — 53(57,59,59) sts.

Change to No. 3 needles.

Row 1: Inc in first st, p 1(3,4,4), (k 6, p 4, k 1, p 3) 3 times, k 6, P2(4,5,5), inc in last st.

Row 2 and All Even Numbered Rows: Knit all knit sts and purl all purl sts as they face you.

Keeping in pat (as given for Back), work 10 rows, **at same time** inc one st at each end of next row and every other row 4 times — 65(69,71,71) sts.

Row 13: Inc in first st, p 0(2,3,3), (k 6, p 4, k 1, p 3) 4 times, k 6, p 1(3,4,4), inc in last st — 67(71,73,73) sts.

Keeping in pat , inc one st at each end of every other row twice, then every 4th row 1(2,5,8) times, working extra sts in pattern whenever possible — 73(79,87,93) sts.

Work even in pat until length measures 5(6,7,8)" from beg, working last row on wrong side.

Cap Shaping:

Bind off 6(6,7,8) sts at beg of next 6 rows.

Bind off rem sts loosely.

LEFT FRONT BAND

Using No. 1 needles, cast on 9 sts.

Row 1: K 2, (p 1, k 1) 3 times, k 1.

Row 2: K 1, (p 1, k 1) 4 times. ***

Rep Rows 1 and 2 39(44,54,59) times.

Break off yarn, leave sts on stitch holder.

RIGHT FRONT BAND

Work as for Left Front Band to ***.

Rep Rows 1 and 2 once.

**** **Row 5:** Rib 4, bind off 2 sts, rib 3.

Row 6: Rib 3, cast on 2 sts, rib 4.

Work 14(16,20,18) rows in rib. ****

Rep from **** to **** 3(3,3,4) times, then Rows 5 and 6 once — 5(5,5,6) button-holes made.

Work 11(13,17,15) rows in rib.

Do not cut yarn, leave sts on needle.

NECKBAND

Sew shoulder seams.

With right side facing and holding Right Front Band sts on needle, use No. 1 needles to pick up and k 73(81,89,97) sts evenly around neck edge, including sts from back neck stitch holder, then rib across Left Front Band sts — 91(99,107,115) sts.

Work 9 rows in rib as for lower band of Back, beg with Row 2 and working a buttonhole (as before) in Rows 4 and 5.

Bind off loosely in rib.

FINISHING

Do not press. Sew in sleeves, placing center of sleeves at shoulder seams, then sew up side and sleeve seams. Sew front bands in place. Sew on buttons.

59

BOOTIES WITH RIBBED ANKLE

TECHNIQUE: Knitting

DIRECTIONS

Using No. 3 needles and Mc, cast on 43 sts.
Work as for Lemon Scented Booties on page 78 to ***.
Work 10 rows st st (k 1 row, p 1 row).
Instep Shaping:
Next Row: K 37 k 2 tog, turn.
Next Row: Sl 1, p 9, p 2 tog, turn.
Next Row: Sl 1, k 9, k 2 tog, turn.
Rep last 2 rows until 45 sts rem (17 sts on each side of instep).
Next Row: Sl 1, k 9, k 2 tog, k 16.
Next Row: Purl — 44 sts.
Ankle:
Next Row: K 1, * yo, k 2 tog, rep from * to last st, k 1.
Next Row: Using A, purl, inc one st at each end — 46 sts.

SIZE

Directions are given for size 0 to 6 months.

NOTE: For slightly smaller booties use one size smaller needles and for slightly larger booties use one size larger needles than suggested to obtain the correct gauge.

MATERIALS

Fingering-Weight Yarn (50 gr. ball): 1 ball each of main color (Mc) and contrasting color (A); 1 pair of No. 3 knitting needles, *or any size needles to obtain gauge below;* 1 yard of $1/4$"-wide ribbon; tapestry needle.

GAUGE

On No. 3 needles in stockinette stitch (st st) — 8 sts = 1"; 11 rows = 1". Be sure to check your gauge.

Next Row: K 2, * p 2, k 2, rep from * to end.
Next Row: P 2, *k 2, p 2, rep from * to end.
Rep last 2 rows until rib section measures $3^1/4$" from beg, working last row on wrong side.
Bind off.

FINISHING

Sew foot and back seam, reversing back seam for $1^1/2$" at ankle edge. Thread ribbon through eyelet holes and tie in a bow. Fold rib section in half onto right side.

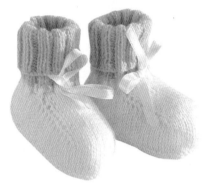

GIANT PINK BUNNY

TECHNIQUE: Sewing

MATERIALS

(about 18" when seated)
- [ ] $1^5/8$ yards of 45"-wide cotton fabric
- [ ] synthetic stuffing
- [ ] embroidery floss
- [ ] black and white felt scraps
- [ ] tracing paper
- [ ] sewing thread

Note: Seam $3/8$" deep with pieces pinned right sides together.

DIRECTIONS
Pattern outline ————————— grey
1 Cutting: Trace full-size patterns, Nos. 23 through 31, including labels. Cut 1 pair each of #23 body front, #25 upper back, #26 side head and #31 upper leg. Cut two #30 soles. Cut one each of #27 head gusset and #24 back lower body and legs

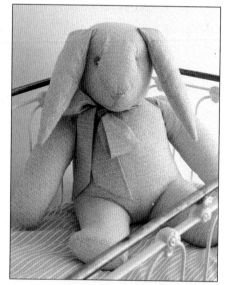

and four each of #28 ears and #29 arms.
2 Head: Stitch the head darts, press them open. Seam side heads from nose down to the larger dart. Matching "noses," seam the gusset between them, leaving a 2" back opening. Turn right side out, stuff it and slipstitch it closed.
3 Back and Front: With a CB edge at each dart edge, seam the short edge of

each upper back to the lower back. Stitch the dart and continue up the CB seam, stopping 2" down from the top point. Seam front bodies at CF edge. With the foot facing outward, baste top of each upper leg to lower edge of front body; stitch.
4 Arms: Seam the straight edge of an arm to each side of the body front, starting 1" down from the top point. Repeat, to match, at back body.
5 Body: Pin front body to back body except at foot bottoms. Clip to crotch corners. Seam a sole to each foot. Turn right side out and stuff. Slipstitch opening closed.
6 Head: Pin head on body and, in a kind of oval sew it by hand along the pins. Seam each pair of ears together except at the short edge. Turn under the raw edge and sew it by hand over a head dart, opening the edge to a shallow oval.
7 Face: Embroider a satin-stitch nose and a chain-stitch mouth (see photo). Contour eye sockets by stitching from one eye to the other with strong thread, pulling it up slightly before you fasten the end. Slipstitch a $1/4$" black circle to a $1/2$" white circle, then slipstitch that to the head (see photo). Repeat.

PILGRIM BONNET

(See photograph page 53, top left)

TECHNIQUE: Sewing
SIZE: 12 months

MATERIALS
- ☐ 1 yard of 45"-wide cotton
- ☐ 1 yard of bias binding
- ☐ 1½ yard of ½"- wide ribbon
- ☐ ¼ yard iron-on interfacing
- ☐ 1¼ yards of eyelet edging

NOTE: Seam ³/₈" deep with the pieces pinned right sides together.

DIRECTIONS
1 Measuring: Measure the head, as follows, in order to draw a pattern like the crown and brim above: *For A to B,* measure from one ear lobe over the head to the opposite ear lobe and add 2". *For X to Y,* measure loosely from center front hairline to nape of neck (about 12").
2 Pattern: Cut a brim pattern like that in the upper corner by drawing a rectangle 8" deep times the A to B measurement established in Step 1. In the crown pattern above, the C to D measurement is twice the A to B length. Cut a piece of paper to

that length times the X to Y measurement in Step 1. Fold the paper in half from X to Y and draw a smooth curve from C to X. Cut through both layers on this curve, then open paper for the crown pattern.
3 Cutting: Cut 1 each of crown and brim. Cut 2 ties each 3" x 16".
4 Eyelet: Pin eyelet to curved edge of crown with right sides together and edges even. Stitch ¼" from the edge, clipping the fabric seam allowance if needed. Press the seam toward the fabric and topstitch close to the seam on the right side.
5 Buttonholes: On the wrong side of the crown, draw a stitching line 1½" from the curved seam. Iron a patch of interfacing (about 3" square) to the wrong side from the X inward and centered on the XY line. Work two ⁵/₈" buttonholes, starting ½" each side of center just below the drawn line (see pattern above).
6 Casing: Stitch the outside edge of bias binding along the drawn line, stretching it slightly. Then stitch the inside edge. Push a 27" length of ribbon through the casing, stitching across one end (near C). Draw the other end out the nearest buttonhole. Repeat from the opposite end (near D).
7 Crown: Sew 2 gathering rows across the crown front ¼" and ³/₈" from the raw edge.
8 Brim: Iron interfacing to wrong side of brim. Fold it in half, right side together, and stitch the short ends. Turn in seam allow-

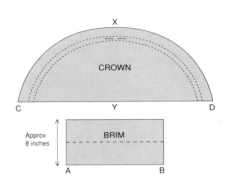

ance on raw edges and press. Turn brim right side out and press.
9 Assembly: Draw up the crown's front edge to fit the brim, having most of the gathering toward the center. Pin the outside brim edge over the gathering and edgestitch without catching in the brim facing. Slipstitch the brim facing to the crown, enclosing the raw edges.
10 Ties: Fold each strip in half lengthwise, right side together. Seam the long edge. Seam one short end at an angle; trim the seam allowance. Turn the tie right side out and press it. At the open end, turn in a seam allowance and press. Then fold a pleat across the end and press. Pin the end inside the bonnet over one end of the casing. Stitch the end securely at 3 edges and across the pleat, making a stitch square.
11 Finishing: Try on the bonnet. Draw up the ribbons to fit and tie them in a bow.

EMBROIDERED SHEET

(See photograph page 52)

TECHNIQUE: Sewing

MATERIALS
- ☐ 2¼ yards of 45"-wide sheer cotton
- ☐ 2⁵/₈ yards of 2"-wide eyelet edging
- ☐ dressmaker's carbon paper
- ☐ small embroidery hoop
- ☐ 6-strand cotton and embroidery needle

DIRECTIONS
1 Pattern: Photocopy or photostat the pattern, enlarging it up to twice its size. Or you can draw floral motifs freehand with a sharp, hard pencil directly on the fabric.
2 Panel: Cut a 4" length of fabric the full

(45") width. With right sides together and edges even, stitch eyelet to the long sides of the panel. Press eyelet outward temporarily, so you have enough fabric to engage the hoop.
3 Embroidery: Centered between the panel ends trace a floral motif, through dressmaker's carbon, to the right side of the fabric. Embroider it, using French knots, buttonhole stitch and back stitch. Add motifs on each side of the center one, as you like.
4 Assembly: At the top edge of the panel turn the eyelet wrong side up again and pin this edge to a 45" end of the sheet. (The right side of the panel should be against the wrong side of the sheet.) Stitch, over the previous stitching, through the 3 layers. Turn panel to the right side, letting the eyelet extend, and press the seamed edge. Topstitch close to both long panel edges and across the raw ends.
5 Finishing: Hem the 2 raw edges of the sheet.

Nursery Pets

A teddy or two and a bunny to cuddle – fill your baby's world with these lovable friends. They can be knitted or sewn, cuddled or worn. We've chosen primary brights for our pet parade but you might prefer pastels or even black and white for a super-sophisticated look.

TEDDY BEAR
SAMPLER

Work this sampler in cross stitch on 14-count Aida cloth, using two strands of floss and following this stitch and color guide.

CROSS STITCH

■	DMC	310	Black
/	DMC	796	Dark Delft Blue
◢	DMC	797	Delft Blue
×	DMC	799	Medium Delft Blue
∩	DMC	800	Pale Delft Blue
—	DMC	972	Yellow
∧	DMC	986	Dark Forest Green
·	DMC	987	Medium Forest Green
T	DMC	989	Forest Green
‡	DMC	433	Brown
⟩	DMC	434	Light Brown

○	DMC	436	Tan
⟍	DMC	437	Light Tan
△	DMC	304	Medium Red
＼	DMC	666	Bright Red

BACKSTITCH

DMC	310	Around ribbon
DMC	304	Lettering
DMC	3031	Bear

RUNNING STITCH

DMC	799	Inside border edge

64

BABY'S OVERALLS AND PULLOVER

TECHNIQUE: Knitting

DIRECTIONS
PULLOVER
BACK
Using No. 3 needles and A, cast on 69(75,81) sts.
Row 1: K 2, * p 1, k 1; rep from * to last st, k 1.
Row 2: K 1, * p 1, k 1; rep from * to end.
Rep Rows 1 and 2, 5(6,7) times more.
Change to No. 5 needles and Mc.
Continue in st st (k 1 row, p 1 row) until work measures 4$\frac{1}{2}$(4$\frac{1}{2}$,5$\frac{1}{2}$)" from beg, ending with a purl row.
Now beg pattern as follows:
Rows 1 and 2: Using A, knit.
Note: When changing colors, pick up new color from under the color being used, twisting yarns on wrong side of work to prevent holes. Carry colors not in use loosely across wrong side of work. Use a separate bobbin for each color change.
Work Rows 3 to 18 following chart A.
Rows 19 and 20: Using A, knit.
Using Mc, work 2 rows in st st.
Armhole Shaping:
Bind off 4 sts at beg of next 2 rows.
Dec one st at each end of every row 5 times — 51(57,63) sts. ******
Work even for 1 row.
Divide for Back Opening:
Row 1: K 28(31,34), turn.
Row 2: K 5, purl to end.
Rep last 2 rows 2(3,3) times more.
Next Row: Knit to last 3 sts, yo, k 2 tog (buttonhole), k 1.
Keeping in garter st border as established, work 11(11,9) rows, then work buttonhole row once. **3rd size only** — rep last 10 rows once more — *2(2,3) buttonholes made.*
Keeping garter st border correct, work 7(7,5) rows.
Shoulder Shaping:
Next Row: Bind off 7(9,10) sts, knit to end.
Next Row: K 5, purl to end.
Next Row: Bind off 8(9,10) sts, knit to end.
Cut yarn and leave rem 13(13,14) sts on stitch holder.
With right side facing, join Mc to rem sts,

SIZE
Directions are given for size 6 months. Changes for 9 months and 12 months are in parentheses.

MATERIALS
Sport-Weight yarn (50 gr. ball): 2 balls of blue (Mc), 1 ball each of red (A) and white (B) for Pullover, 3(3,4) balls of Mc, 1 ball each of (A) and (B) for Overalls; 1 pair each No. 3 and No. 5 knitting needles, *or any size needles to obtain gauge below*; 3 stitch holders; 3(3,4) buttons, bobbins for Pullover; 1 stitch holder, 4 buttons, bobbins, length of elastic for Overalls; tapestry needle.

GAUGE
On No. 5 needles in stockinette stitch (st st) — 13 sts = 2"; 9 rows = 1". Be sure to check your gauge.

MEASUREMENTS

Sizes (mos.):	6	9	12
Body Chest:	18"	20"	22"
Finished Measurements:			
Pullover Chest:	20"	22"	24"
Length to Back Neck:			
	10$\frac{1}{2}$"	11"	12$\frac{1}{2}$"
Sleeve Length:			
	6"	7$\frac{1}{2}$"	8"
Overall Inner Leg Length (excluding cuff):			
	7"	8"	9$\frac{1}{2}$"
Outer Leg Length to Beg of Ribbed Waist (excluding cuff):			
	15"	16"	17"

cast on 5 sts (for underlap) and complete to correspond with other side, omitting buttonholes.
FRONT
Work as for Back to ******.
Work 13(13,17) rows in st st.
Neck Shaping:
Using Mc, k 19(22,25), turn.
Dec one st at neck edge every other row 4(4,5) times — 15(18,21) sts.
Work even for 5(7,7) rows in st st.
Shoulder Shaping:
Bind off 7(9,10) sts at beg of next row.

Work even for 1 row.
Bind off.
Slip next 13 sts onto a stitch holder and leave for front neck. Join Mc to rem sts and complete to correspond with other side.
SLEEVES
Using No. 3 needles and A, cast on 39(41,41) sts.
Work 10(12,14) rows in rib as given for lower band of Back, inc 2(4,6) sts evenly across last row — 41(45,47) sts.
Change to No. 5 needles.
Row 1: Using A, inc in first st, knit to last st, inc in last st.
Row 2: Knit.
Work Rows 3 to 18 following chart B, **at the same time**, inc one st at each end of 7th(5th,3rd) row once, then every 8th(6th,4th) row once, **3rd size only** — then in foll 6th row once — 47(51,55) sts.
Using A, knit 2 rows in garter st.
Using Mc and working in st st, inc one st at each end of 5th(next,next) row once, then every 8th(8th,6th) row 1(2,4) times — 51(57,65) sts.
Work even until side edge measures 6 (7$\frac{1}{2}$,8)" from beg, ending with a purl row.
Cap Shaping:
Bind off 2 sts at beg of next 2 rows.
Dec one st at each end of next and every other row 7(6,7) times, then in every row until 13(13,15) sts rem.
Bind off.
NECKBAND
Sew shoulder seams.
With right side facing, using No. 3 needles and A, beg at left back opening, knit across 13(13,14) sts on left back neck stitch holder, pick up and k 13(15,17) sts evenly along left side of neck, k across 13 sts from front stitch holder, pick up and k 13(15,17) sts evenly along right side of neck, k across 13(13,14) sts on right back neck stitch

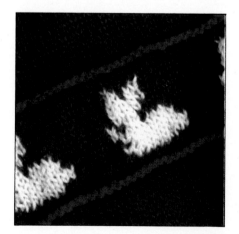

holder — 65(69,75) sts.

Row 1: K 5, * p 1, k 1; rep from * to last 6 sts, p 1, k 5.

Row 2: K 5, rib to last 5 sts, k 2, yo, k 2 tog (buttonhole), k 1.

Keeping in garter st borders as established, work 3 rows in rib.

Bind off loosely in rib.

FINISHING

Sew side and sleeve seams, then sew in sleeves. Sew on buttons.

OVERALLS — PANTS
RIGHT LEG

Beg at waist, using No. 3 needles and Mc, cast on 91(101,109) sts loosely.

Work 8(10,10) rows in rib as for lower band of Pullover Back.

Change to No. 5 needles.

Work 2 rows st st (k 1 row, p 1 row).

Note: To avoid holes when turning, bring yarn to front of work, slip next st onto right-hand needle, with yarn in back of work, slip st back onto left-hand needle, then turn and proceed as instructed.

Row 1: K 16, turn.

Row 2 and All Even Numbered Rows: Purl.

Row 3: K 22, turn.

Row 5: K 28, turn.

Continue turning in this manner, working 6 more sts in every knit row until the Row "k 52(58,64), turn" has been worked.

Next Row: Rep Row 2.

Cont until short side measures 8(8¼,8½)" from beg, ending with a purl row.

Crotch Shaping:

Bind off 3 sts at beg of next 2 rows — 85(95,103) sts.

Cont in st st until work measures 2½ (4½,8)" from crotch shaping, ending with a purl row.

Using A, knit 2 rows in garter st.

Note: When changing colors pick up new color from under the color being used, twisting yarns on wrong side of work to prevent holes. Carry colors not in use loosely across wrong side of work. Use a separate bobbin for each color change.

Work rows 3 to 18 following chart C.

Rows 19 and 20: Using A, knit.

Using Mc, work 2 rows in st st, dec 12(14,16) sts evenly across last row — 73(81,87) sts.

Change to No. 3 needles.

Work 28 rows in rib as for waistband.

Bind off loosely in rib.

LEFT LEG

Work to correspond with Right Leg.

Sew center front seam and center back seam of pants.

FRONT BODICE

Using No. 5 needles and Mc, cast on 39(43,49) sts loosely.

Work 4(6,8) rows in st st.

Using A, knit 2 rows in garter st.

Work Rows 3 to 18 following chart D.

Using A, knit 2 rows in garter st.

Using Mc, work 2(4,4) rows in st st.

Leave sts on stitch holder.

SIDE STRIPS (Make 2)

Using No. 3 needles and A, cast on 8 sts.

Cont in garter st (Row 1 is wrong side) until strip measures same length as Front Bodice, working last row on wrong side.

Leave sts on spare needle.

TOP BORDER OF BODICE

Using No. 3 needles and A, knit across first side strip, knit across sts on Front Bodice stitch holder, knit across a second side strip — 55(59,65) sts.

Knit 9 rows in garter st.

Bind off.

BACK BODICE

Using No. 5 needles and Mc, cast on

39(43,49) sts loosely.

Work 40(50,58) rows in st st.

Leave sts on stitch holder

SIDE STRIPS (Make 2)

Using No. 3 needles and A, cast on 8 sts.

Cont in garter st (Row 1 is wrong side) until strip measures same length as Back Bodice, working last row on wrong side.

Leave sts on spare needle.

TOP BORDER OF BODICE

Using No. 3 needles and A, knit across first side strip, knit across sts on Back stitch holder, knit across second side strip — 55(59,65) sts.

Knit 9 rows in garter st.

Divide for shoulder straps:

Next Row: K 15(16,18), bind off 25(27,29), k 15(16,18).

Cont on last 15(16,18) sts until shoulder strap measures 3½(4,5)" from beg. Divide for Shoulder Straps, working last row on wrong side.

Next Row: K 3, k 2 tog, yo, k 5(6,8), yo, k 2 tog, k 3.

Knit 5 rows in garter st.

Bind off.

Join A to rem sts and complete as for other Shoulder Strap.

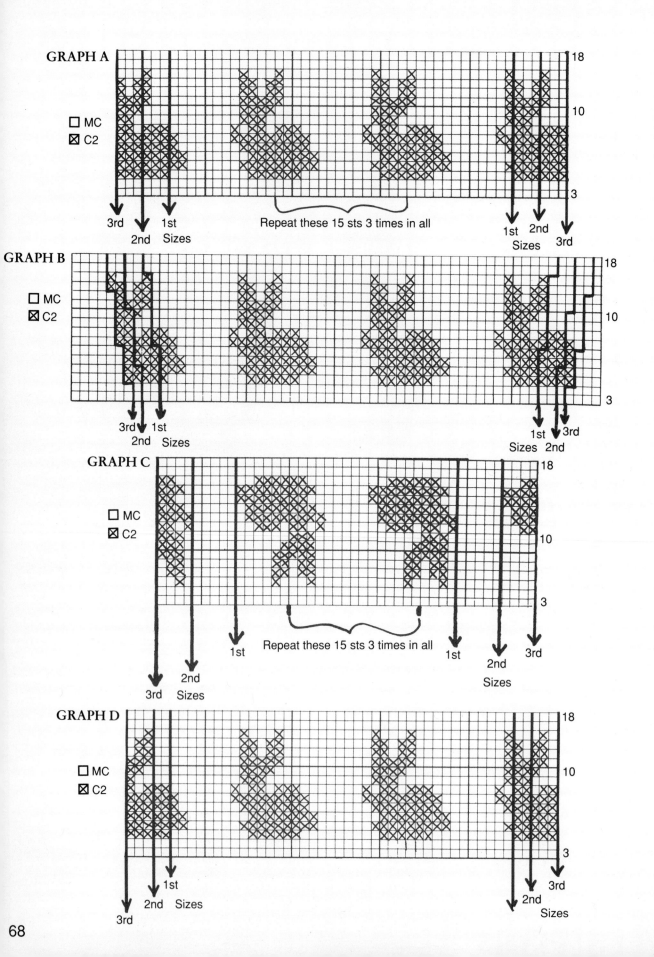

GRAPH A

☐ MC
☒ C2

18
10
3

3rd   1st
2nd   Sizes

Repeat these 15 sts 3 times in all

1st   2nd
Sizes   3rd

GRAPH B

☐ MC
☒ C2

18
10
3

3rd   1st
2nd   Sizes

1st   3rd
Sizes   2nd

GRAPH C

☐ MC
☒ C2

18
10
3

1st   Repeat these 15 sts 3 times in all   1st

3rd
2nd
Sizes

2nd
Sizes   3rd

GRAPH D

☐ MC
☒ C2

18
10
3

1st
2nd   Sizes

3rd

2nd   3rd
Sizes

FINISHING

Press lightly on wrong side, using a warm iron and damp cloth, if desired. Sew leg seams, reversing seam for 1" at lower edge for cuff. Sew Back and Front side strips to side edges of Bodices. Sew Back and Front Bodice to center Back and Front of Overall Pants (matching rib stitches of Overall, so that pants will slip over baby easily). Thread elastic through 3 rows of rib at waist (if desired), using narrow, flat elastic or round elastic. Sew buttons to Front Bodice to match buttonholes on Shoulder Straps.

POLKA DOT SUNSUIT

TECHNIQUE: Sewing

SIZE: 0 to 6 months

MATERIALS

- ☐ ¹/₂ yard of 45"-wide polka dot cotton fabric
- ☐ ¹/₂ yard of 45"-wide white pique fabric
- ☐ scrap of white fabric for bunny appliqué
- ☐ 11 hammer-on snaps or velcro dots
- ☐ 1 yard of ³/₈"-wide elastic
- ☐ small amt. of fusible interfacing for appliqué
- ☐ tracing paper and pencil
- ☐ sewing thread to match fabric

NOTE: The sunsuit is a fully lined, one-piece garment, snapped at bloomer sides and center front. To "cut a pair," pin the pattern to folded fabric. Seam ³/₈" deep with pieces pinned right sides together.

DIRECTIONS

Pattern outline • • • • • • • • • • • • • • • • • •

1   Pattern: Trace the full-size patterns Nos. 5 and 6 (see pull-out sheet and pattern outline above) including all marks and labels.

2   Cutting: From the dotted and the white fabrics, cut one pair each of #5 upper fronts and, with the long CB/CF centerline on a fold of fabric, one each of #6 back and bloomers.

3   Appliqué: Use the pattern on page 32 and follow the directions in Step 3.

4   Lining: Seam upper fronts to the back and bloomers piece at the shoulder edges. Repeat for lining. Pin suit to lining, right sides together, and stitch around all edges except at the straight bottom (waist) edge. Clip to the black dot at each underarm and clip the curved edges. Turn right side out and press. Edgestitch.

5   Leg Casing: From A to B stitch ¹/₈" from the edge of each leg opening. Stitch again ¹/₂" away to make a casing. Insert 12"-long elastic into each casing and stitch 2 or 3 times across each end.

6   Waist Casing: Pin the raw edges together and overcast them with machine zigzag. Turn the edge ⁵/₈" to the wrong side, press, and stitch the casing. Insert 7" of elastic through the casing and pin both ends. Smooth out the fabric at each end and stitch 2 or 3 times through the elastic ⁵/₈" from a side edge. Pull out the elastic ends and trim off the excess. Stitch the casing ends closed.

7   Snaps: Following the manufacturer's directions, apply 3 snaps to the front (at the 3 circles) and at the bloomer sides (at the 3 lower circles). Then apply 1 snap at the side of each front (under the arm) to meet the top circle above the bloomer closing.

69

TEDDY BEAR QUILT

TECHNIQUE: Sewing

It looks complicated but is so simple! This quilt is made with a purchased baby quilt panel, available at many craft stores. Choose a complementary fabric for the quiltback, cut 1" larger all around than the quilttop (you will turn over edges twice to bind the top). Pin the edges of the panel to a same-sized piece of synthetic batting, center that over the wrong side of the quiltback and baste the layers together. Hand-stitch around the motif outlines. An embroidery hoop will make this much easier. Stitch along the vertical and horizontal lines of the panel as well, to give the effect of quilting. You can use matching or contrasting sewing thread, depending on the effect you want to create.

GIANT RED BUNNY

TECHNIQUE: Sewing

MATERIALS
(about 18" when seated)
- [ ] 1⅝ yards of 45"-wide cotton fabric
- [ ] synthetic stuffing
- [ ] embroidery floss
- [ ] black and white felt scraps
- [ ] tracing paper
- [ ] sewing thread

NOTE: Seam ³/₈" deep with pieces pinned right sides together.

DIRECTIONS
Pattern outline —————— grey
1 Cutting: Trace full-size patterns, Nos. 23 through 31, including labels. Cut 1 pair each of #23 body front, #25 upper back, #26 side head and #31 upper leg. Cut two #30 soles. Cut one each of #27 head gusset and #24 back lower body and legs and four each of #28 ears and #29 arms.
2 Head: Stitch the head darts, press them open. Seam side heads from nose down to the larger dart. Matching "noses,"

seam the gusset between them, leaving a 2" back opening. Turn right side out, stuff it and slipstitch it closed.
3 Back and Front: With a CB edge at each dart edge, seam the short edge of each upper back to the lower back. Stitch the dart and continue up the CB seam, stopping 2" down from the top point. Seam front bodies at CF edge. With the foot facing outward, baste top of each upper

leg to lower edge of front body; stitch.
4 Arms: Seam the straight edge of an arm to each side of the body front, starting 1" down from the top point. Repeat, to match, at back body.
5 Body: Pin front body to back body except at foot bottoms. Clip to crotch corners. Seam a sole to each foot. Turn right side out and stuff. Slipstitch opening closed.
6 Head: Pin head on body and, in a kind of oval sew it by hand along the pins. Seam each pair of ears together except at the short edge. Turn under the raw edge and sew it by hand over a head dart, opening the edge to a shallow oval.
7 Face: Embroider a satin-stitch nose and a chain-stitch mouth (see photo). Contour eye sockets by stitching from one eye to the other with strong thread, pulling it up slightly before you fasten the end. Slipstitch a ¹/₄" black circle to a ¹/₂" white circle, then slipstitch that to the head (see photo). Repeat.

Note: *When making toys for babies and small children use felt or embroidered eyes for safety. Buttons and plastic eyes can be pulled loose and swallowed by little ones. Make sure any trims you use are sewn on very securely. Give them a good tug just to make sure they won't come off.*

BABY BEARS

TECHNIQUE: Sewing

MATERIALS

- ☐ ¼ yard of 45"-wide cotton fabric
- ☐ synthetic stuffing
- ☐ scraps of felt for eyes
- ☐ embroidery floss
- ☐ paper or thin cardboard for pattern

NOTE: Seam ³⁄₈" deep with right sides together. Clip seam allowance at curves.

DIRECTIONS

1 Pattern: Enlarge pattern pieces (below) to actual size and add ³⁄₈" seam allowances all around. Cut out 1 pair (2) or 2 pairs (4) from folded fabric.

2 Sew each pair of arm and leg pieces together, leaving upper straight edge open. Turn and stuff firmly.

3 Sew each pair of body sections together along one curved edge. Sew two halves of body together, leaving neck edge open. Turn and stuff firmly.

4 Sew ear pieces together around curved edge. Turn. Stuff lightly. Sew center front and back head seams. Join front and back head. Turn and stuff firmly.

5 Using doubled thread, gather neck edge of body. Pull up and secure.

6 Pin arms, legs, head and ears to body turning under the raw edge. Slipstitch securely.

7 Fasten around felt eyes to head with buttonhole stitch. Embroider nose in satin stitch, and mouth in chain or stem stitch.

BABY BEAR GRID PATTERN

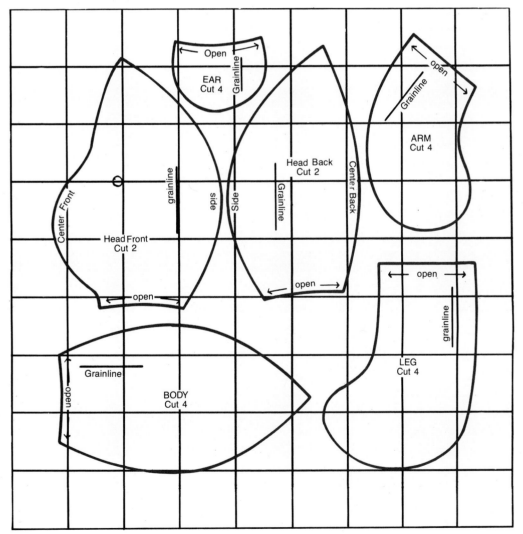

Each square is 1 inch x 1 inch.

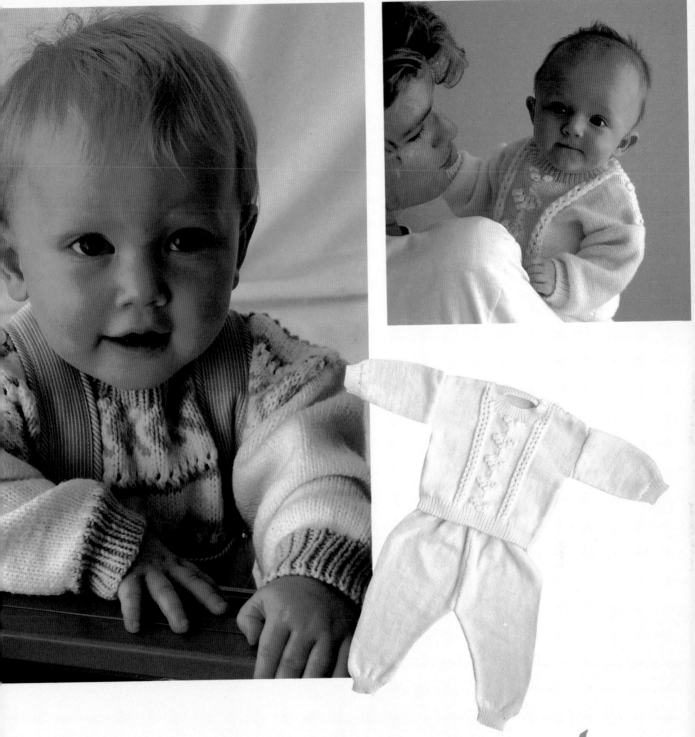

Lemon Scented

Whether the stork delivers a baby boy or girl, you'll be prepared with this collection of pretty lemon knits. Team a precious pullover with the neatest pair of cuffed overalls you'll ever see. And gather it all up into the wonderful carry-all bag which doubles as a changing pad.

FAIR ISLE PULLOVER AND OVERALLS

TECHNIQUE: Knitting

PULLOVER
BACK
Using No. 2 needles and A, cast on 69(77,85) sts.
Row 1: K 2, * p 1, k 1; rep from * to last st, k 1.
Row 2: K 1, * p 1, k 1; rep from * to end.
Rep Rows 1 and 2 until lower band measures 1¼" from beg, ending with Row 2.
Change to No. 4 needles.
Row 1: Using Mc, k 1, * yo, k 2 tog; rep from * to end.
Work 3 rows in st st (k 1 row, p 1 row), beg with a purl row.
Change to No. 5 needles.
Note: When changing colors pick up new color from under the color being used, twisting yarns on wrong side to prevent holes. Carry color not in use loosely across wrong side of work. Always carry colors to end of row.
** Row 5: K 1 A, * k 2 Mc, k 2 A; rep from * to end.
Row 6: P 1 Mc, * p 2 A, p 2 Mc; rep from * to end.
Row 7: K 1 Mc, * k 2 A, k 2 Mc; rep from * to end.
Row 8: P 1 A, * p 2 Mc, p 2 A; rep from * to end.
Row 9: * K 2 A, k 2 Mc; rep from * to last st, k 1 A.
Row 10: * P 2 Mc, p 2 A; rep from * to last st, p 1 Mc.
Row 11: * K 2 Mc, k 2 A; rep from * to last st, k 1 Mc.
Row 12: * P 2 A, p 2 Mc; rep from * to last st, p 1 A.
Change to No. 4 needles.
Using Mc, work 2 rows in st st.
Using B, work 2 rows in st st.
Row 17: Using Mc, rep Row 1.
Row 18: Purl.
Row 19: Using A, * sl 1, k 1, psso, yo; rep from * to last st, k 1.
Row 20: Purl.
Using Mc, work 2 rows in st st.
Change to No. 5 needles.
Row 23: K 3 Mc, * k 7 B, k 1 Mc; rep from * to last 2 sts, k 2 Mc.
Row 24: P 4 Mc, * p 5 B, p 3 Mc; rep from

* to last 9 sts, p 5 B, p 4 Mc.
Row 25: K 5 Mc, * k 3 B, k 5 Mc; rep from * to end.
Row 26: P 6 Mc, * p 1 B, p 7 Mc; rep from * to last 7 sts, p 1 B, p 6 Mc.
Change to No. 4 needles.
Rows 27-30: Using Mc, work 2 rows in st st.
Using A, work 2 rows in st st.
Row 31: Using Mc, rep Row 1.
Row 32: Purl.
Row 33: Using B, rep Row 19.
Row 34: Purl.
Using Mc, work 2 rows in st st.
Change to No. 5 needles. ******
Rep from ** to ** for pattern.
Continue in pat until work measures 9(10,11½)" from beg, working last row on wrong side.
Shoulder Shaping:
Keeping in pat, bind off 7(9,10) sts at beg of next 4 rows, then 8(8,9) sts at beg of next 2 rows.
Leave rem 25(25,27) sts on a stitch holder for back neck.
FRONT
Work as given for Back until there are 16(16,18) rows less than Back to shoulder shaping.
Neck Shaping:
Next Row: Work in pat across 28(32,36), turn.
*** Keeping in pat, dec one st at neck edge in every row until 22(26,29) sts rem.
Work even for 3(3,4) rows ***.
Note: This side of neck is shorter to accommodate shoulder band.
Shoulder Shaping:
Keeping in pat, bind off 7(9,10) sts at beg

SIZE
Directions are given for size 3 months. Changes for 6 months and 9 months are in parentheses.

MATERIALS
Fingering-Weight yarn (50 gr. ball): 2(2,3) balls of white (Mc), 2 balls of blue (A) and and 1 ball of yellow (B) for Pullover; 4(4,5) balls of A for Overalls; 1 pair each No. 2, No. 4 and No. 5 knitting needles, *or any size needles to obtain gauge below*; 2 stitch holders and 3 buttons for Pullover; length of elastic and 2 buttons for Overalls; tapestry needle.

GAUGE
On No. 4 needles in stockinette stitch (st st) — 15 sts = 2"; 10 rows = 1". Be sure to check your gauge.

MEASUREMENTS

Sizes (mos.):	3	6	9
Body Chest:	16"	18"	20"
Finished Measurements:			
Pullover Chest:	18"	20"	22"
Length to Back Neck:			
	9"	10"	12"
Sleeve Length:			
	5½"	6½"	8"
Overalls Outer Leg Length:			
	12¼"	13¼"	14½"

Cuddly toys are always a special favorite and will continue to be much-loved for many years. Make this baby-sized teddy bear following the pattern and instructions on page 71. Choose a pretty printed cotton, velveteen or felt for the bear and stuff it with lightweight polyester fiber. Loose buttons and beads are very dangerous so always embroider or paint features on (with non-toxic paint) and make sure all ribbons and trims are very well secured.

of next row and every other row once.

Work even for 1 row.

Bind off.

Slip next 13 sts onto stitch holder for front neck.

Join yarn to rem sts and work in pat to end.

Work as given from *** to ***.

Work even for 7 rows.

Shoulder Shaping:
Complete as for other Shoulder Shaping.

SLEEVES
Using No. 2 needles and A, cast on 37(37,39) sts.

Work in rib as for lower band of Back, until band measures 1¼" from beg, ending with Row 2 and inc 8 sts evenly across last row — 45(45,47) sts.

Change to No. 4 needles and Mc.

Work in st st, inc one st at each end of 5th, then every other row until there are 51(55, 57) sts, then every 4th row until there are 61(67,73) sts.

Work even until length measures 5½ (6½,8)" from beg, ending with a purl row.

Cap Shaping:
Bind off 5(5,6) sts at beg of next 8 rows.

Bind off rem sts.

NECKBAND
Sew right shoulder seam. With right side facing, using No. 2 needles and A, pick up and k 71(71,75) sts evenly around neck edge (including sts from stitch holders).

Work 7 rows rib as for lower band of Back, beg with Row 2.

Bind off loosely in rib.

LEFT FRONT SHOULDER BAND
With right side facing, using No. 2 needles and A, pick up and k 31(35,39) sts evenly along Left Front Shoulder and side edge of Neckband.

Work 3 rows in rib as given for lower band of Back, beg with Row 2.

Row 4: Rib 3(4,6) [k 2 tog, yo, rib 10(11,12)] twice, k 2 tog, yo, rib 2(3,3) — *3 button-holes made.*

Work 3 rows in rib.

Bind off loosely in rib.

LEFT BACK SHOULDER BAND
Work as for Left Front Shoulder Band, omitting buttonholes.

FINISHING
Press lightly on wrong side with a damp iron if desired. Overlap front shoulder band over back shoulder band and stitch in place at armhole edge.

Sew in sleeves, placing center of sleeve at shoulder seams. Join side and sleeve seams. Sew on buttons.

OVERALLS
RIGHT LEG
Beg at waist, using No. 2 needles and A, cast on 81(85,89) sts.

Row 1: K 2, * p 1, k 1; rep from * to last st, k 1.

Row 2: K 1, * p 1, k 1; rep from * to end. Rep Rows 1 and 2 until work measures 2" from beg, ending with Row 2 and inc one st at end of last row — 82(86,90) sts.

Change to No. 4 needles.

Work 2 rows in st st (k 1 row, p 1 row).

Back Shaping:
Note: To avoid holes when turning, bring yarn to front of work, slip next st onto right-hand needle, with yarn in back, slip st back on to left-hand needle, then turn and proceed as instructed. ****

Row 1: K 14(16,18), turn.

Row 2 and All Even Numbered Rows: Purl.

Row 3: K 21(23,25), turn.

Row 5: K 28(30,32), turn.

Row 7: K 35(37,39), turn.

Row 9: K 42(44,46), turn.

Continue turning in this manner, working 7 more sts every other row until the Row

"k 70(72,74) turn" has been worked.

Next Row: Purl.

***** Continue in st st, inc one st at each end of 11th and foll 10th(12th,14th) row until there are 88(92,96) sts.

Work even until length of shorter edge measures 6¼(6½,7½)" from beg, ending with a purl row.

Mark end of last row for back edge.

Leg Shaping:
Dec one st at each end of next row, then every 3rd row until 58(66,86) sts rem, then every 4th row until 56(60,64) sts rem.

Continue in st st until side edge measures 6¼(6¾,7¾)" from marker, ending with a purl row and dec 13 sts evenly across last row — 43(47,51) sts.

Change to No. 2 needles.

Work 12 rows in rib as given for waist.

Bind off loosely in rib. *****

LEFT LEG
Beg at waist, work as given for Right Leg to ****.

Row 1 and All Odd Numbered Rows: Knit

Row 2: P 14(16,18), turn.

Row 4: P 21(23,25), turn.

Row 6: P 28(30,32), turn.
Row 8: P 35(37,39), turn.
Row 10: P 42(44,46), turn.
Continue turning in this manner, working 7 sts more every other row until the row "p 70(72,74), turn" has been worked.
Work as given from ***** to ***** placing marker at beg of corresponding row, instead of at the end.

BIB

Sew center front and center back seams. Place a marker half way between center front and center back seams on each side of waist ribbing.
With right side facing, using No. 4 needles and A, beg 1¼" in from marker, pick up and k 53(59,65) sts evenly to within 1¼" of other marker.
Row 1: K 3, purl to last 3 sts, k 3.
Row 2: Knit.
Rep Rows 1 and 2 until work measures 3½(4,5)" from beg, ending with Row 2.

Work 2 rows in rib as given for lower band of Pullover.
Next Row: Rib 8, yo, k 2 tog, rib to last 10 sts, k 2 tog, yo, rib 8.
Work 3 rows in rib.
Bind off loosely in rib.
STRAPS (make two)
Using No. 2 needles and A, cast on 17 sts. Work in rib as given for lower band of Pullover, until strap measures 7½(9½,10)" from beg, ending with Row 2.
Bind off loosely in rib.

FINISHING

Sew leg seams. Thread elastic through rows of rib at waist as desired. Sew straps in place at back of Overalls. Cross straps. Sew on buttons.

BLUE STRIPED OVERALLS

TECHNIQUE: Sewing

SIZE: 6 to 12 months

MATERIALS

☐ 1 yard of 45"-wide cotton fabric
☐ 5" x 12" iron-on interfacing
☐ ⅛"-wide piping cord (4½ yards)
☐ two ½"-wide buttons
☐ 12" of ⅝"-wide elastic
☐ tracing paper and pencil

NOTE: To "cut a pair," pin the pattern to folded fabric. Seam ⅜" deep with pieces pinned right sides together.

DIRECTIONS
Pattern outline — — — — — — —
1 **Cutting:** Trace full-size patterns, Nos. 19, 20 and 20a (see pullout sheet and pattern outline above). With its CF line on a fold of fabric, cut two #19 bibs. Cut one pair each of #20 pants and #20a leg facings. Cut two each of straps and strap facings, each 2" x 20". Cut a 3" x 11½" back casing and a 4" x 6" pocket and about 4½ yards (pieced on the straight grain) of 1½"-wide

bias strips to cover piping cord.
2 **Preparations:** Iron interfacing to wrong side of a bib piece; trim edges flush. Fold the bias strip over the cord, right side out and raw edges even, and stitch with a zipper foot through both layers against the cord.
3 **Pocket:** With right side together, turn over 2" to make a square; seam down both short ends. Turn it right side out, turn under raw edges, press and edgestitch pocket to one overall piece (see pattern).
4 **Pants:** Seam #20 pieces together at the back crotch, then front crotch edges. Fold the piece so the seams are matched

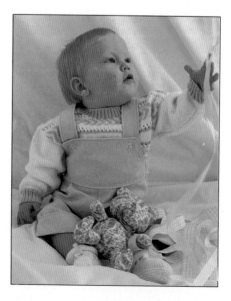

and centered, then stitch the inner leg seams. With raw edges even, baste piping over the bottom edge of each pant leg. Seam short ends of each leg facing and pin it over the piping, with seams matching; stitch. Turn facings inside, hem them and turn up the cuffs. At the waist, fold and baste the pleats (see pattern). Stitch piping to pants, raw edges even.
5 **Bib:** Baste piping over the curved, top edges of the bib, raw edges even. Stitch facing on top, right sides together. Turn and press; topstitch in the piping seam.
6 **Casing:** With lower edges even and right sides together, stitch one end of the casing to each side edge of the bib. Stitch them both to the pants, matching CF's. Turn up the raw edge of casing ¼", fold it down just beyond the waist seam and stitch. Thread elastic through the casing and stitch twice across each end, adjusting its length to fit. Press raw edges toward bib; turn under raw edge of bib facing and slipstitch.
7 **Straps:** Pipe and face the straps, leaving one end open. Turn, press and topstitch. Crossing the straps diagonally, pin each open end to the back casing; stitch securely. Make two buttonholes (see pattern) and sew a button to each strap.

Blue Striped Overalls, Fair Isle Pullover. Make the little floral teddy in exactly the same manner as the one on page 71.

PULLOVER AND PANTS

TECHNIQUE: Knitting

DIRECTIONS
BACK
Using No. 2 needles, cast on 69(75,83) sts.

Row 1 (right side): K 2, * p 1, k 1; rep from * to last st, k 1.

Row 2: K 1, * p 1, k 1; rep from * to end.
Rep Rows 1 and 2 until band measures 1¼" from beg, ending with Row 2.
Change to No. 4 needles.
Continue in rev st st until work measures 8½(10,11½)" from beg, ending with a k row.

Shoulder Shaping:
Bind off 8(9,10) sts at beg of next 4 rows, then 8(8,9) sts at beg of next 2 rows.
Leave rem 21(23,25) sts on a stitch holder for back neck.

FRONT
Using No. 2 needles, cast on 71(79,87) sts.

Continue in rib as for lower band of Back until band measures 1¼" from beg, ending with Row 2.
Change to No. 4 needles.

Row 1 (right side): P 19(23,27), k 2 tog, yo, k 3, p 23, k 2 tog, yo, k 3, p 19(23,27).

Row 2: K 19(23,27), p 5, k 23, p 5, k 19(23,27).

Row 3: P 19(23,27), k 3, yo, k 2 tog, p 11, Bobble, p 11, k 3, yo, k 2 tog, p 19(23,27).

Row 4: K 19(23,27), p 5, k 11, p 1, k 11, p 5, k 19(23,27).

Row 5: P 19(23,27), k 2 tog, yo, k 3, p 8, Bobble, p 2, k 1, p 2, Bobble, p 8, k 2 tog, yo, k 3, p 19(23, 27).

Row 6: K 19(23,27), p 5, k 8, p 1, k 2, p 1, k 2, p 1, k 8, p 5, k 19(23, 27).

Row 7: P 19(23,27), k 3, yo, k 2 tog, p 6, Bobble, p 1, FC, p 1, K1B, p 1, BC, p 1, Bobble, p 6, k 3, yo, k 2 tog, p 19(23,27).

Row 8: K 19(23,27), p 5, k 6, p 1, k 2,(p 1, k 1) 3 times, k 1, p 1, k 6, p 5, k 19(23,27).

Row 9: P 19(23,27), k 2 tog, yo, k 3, p 6, FC, p 1, FC, k 1, BC, p 1, BC, p 6, k 2 tog, yo, k 3, p 19(23,27).

Row 10: K 19(23,27), p 5, k 7, BC, k 1, p 3, k 1, FC, k 7, p 5, k 19(23,27).

Row 11: P 19(23,27), k 3, yo, k 2 tog, p 8, FC, Ml, sl1, k 2 tog, psso, Ml, BC, p 8, k 3, yo, k 2 tog, p 19(23,27).

Row 12: K 19(23,27), p 5, k 9, BC, p 1, FC, k 9, p 5, k 19(23,27).

Row 13: P 19(23,27), k 2 tog, yo, k 3, p 9, purl into front and back of next st, sl1, k 2 tog, psso, purl into front and back of next st, p 9, k 2 tog, yo, k 3, p 19(23,27).

Row 14: K 19(23,27), p 5, k 11, p 1, k 11, p 5, k 19(23,27).

Row 15: P 19(23,27), k 3, yo, k 2 tog, p 23, k 3, yo, k 2 tog, p 19 (23,27).

Row 16: Rep Row 2.
Rows 1 to 16 form pattern.
Cont in pat until there are 16(18,18) rows less than Back to shoulder shaping.

Neck Shaping:
Next Row: Work in pat across 28(32,35), turn.
** Keeping in pat, dec one st at neck edge every other row until 24(26,29) sts rem.**
Work even for 1 row.
Note: This side of neck is 6 rows lower to accommodate Left Front Shoulder Band.
Shoulder Shaping:
Keeping in pat, bind off 8(9, 10) sts at beg of next row and every other row.
Work even for 1 row.
Bind off.
Slip next 15(15,17) sts onto a stitch holder for front neck and leave. Join yarn to rem sts and work in pat to end.
Rep from ** to **
Work even for 8(6,6) rows.
Shoulder Shaping:
Complete as for other shoulder.
SLEEVES
Using No. 2 needles, cast on 39(43,45) sts.

Continue in rib as for lower band of Back until band measures 1¼" from beg, ending with Row 2 and inc 10 sts evenly across last row — 49(53,55) sts.
Change to No. 4 needles.

SIZE
Directions are given for size 3 months. Changes for 6 months and 9 months are in parentheses.

MATERIALS
Fingering-Weight yarn (50 gr. ball): 4(4,5) balls for Pullover; 3(3,4) balls for Pants; 1 pair each No. 2 and No. 4 knitting needles, *or any size needles to obtain gauge below*; 2 stitch holders; 3 buttons; a cable needle for Pullover; elastic for pants; tapestry needle.

GAUGE
On No. 4 needles in stockinette stitch (st st) — 15 sts = 2"; 10 rows = 1". Be sure to check your gauge.

MEASUREMENTS
Sizes (mos.):	3	6	9
Body Chest:	16"	18"	20"
Finished Measurements:			
Pullover Chest:	17¾"	19¾"	21¾"
Length to Back Neck:			
	9"	10"	12"
Sleeve Length:			
	5"	6"	7"
Pants Outer Leg Length:			
	12"	13½"	14½"

STITCHES
Reverse Stockinette Stitch (rev st st): P on right side, k on wrong side.
Bobble: [(k 1, p 1) twice, k 1], all in next st, turn, p 5, turn, k 5, slip 2nd, 3rd, 4th and 5th sts over first st.
FC: Slip next st onto a cable needle and hold in front of work, p 1, then k 1 from cable needle.
BC: Slip next st onto a cable needle, hold in back of work, k 1, then p 1 from cable needle.
Ml: Pick up loop which lies between next st, place on left hand needle, purl into back of it.
K1B: Knit one below, knitting both loops at same time.

Continue in rev st st, inc one st at each end of 3rd row and every 4th(4th,6th) row until there are 61(63,65) sts, **2nd and 3rd sizes only** — then every (6th, 8th) row until there are (67,69) sts.
Work even until length measures 5(6,7)" from beg, ending with a knit row.

Cap Shaping:
Bind off 8(9,10) sts at beg of next 4 rows, then 9(10,9) sts at beg of foll 2 rows. Bind off rem sts.

NECKBAND

Sew right shoulder seam. With right side facing, using No. 2 needles, beg at left front shoulder seam, pick up and k 69(75,79) sts evenly around neck edge (including sts from stitch holder).
Continue in rib as for lower band of Back (beg with Row 2) until band measures ³/₄" from beg ending with Row 2. Bind off loosely in rib.

LEFT FRONT SHOULDER BAND

With right side facing, using No. 2 needles, pick up and k 25(29,33) sts evenly along left front shoulder edge.
Work 1 row in rib as for lower band of Back.
Next Row: Rib 2, [bind off 2 sts, rib 7(9,11)] twice, bind off 2 sts, rib 3.
Next Row: Rib 3 [cast on 2 sts, rib 7(9,11)] twice, cast on 2 sts, rib 2 — *3 buttonholes made.*
Work 2 rows in rib. Bind off loosely in rib.

LEFT BACK SHOULDER BAND

Work as for Left Front Shoulder Band omitting buttonholes.

FINISHING

Overlap Left Front Shoulder Band over Left Back Shoulder Band, and slip stitch together at side edge. Sew in sleeves placing center of sleeves at shoulders. Sew on buttons.

PANTS

RIGHT LEG

Beg at waist, using No. 2 needles, cast on 81(85,89) sts.
Row 1: K 2, * p 1, k 1; rep from * to last st, k 1.
Row 2: K 1, * p 1, k 1; rep from * to end.
Rep Rows 1 and 2 twice, inc one st in center of last row — 82(86,90) sts.
Change to No. 4 needles.
Work 2 rows in st st (k 1 row, p 1 row).

Back Shaping:
Note: To avoid holes when turning, bring yarn to front of work, slip next st onto right-hand needle, with yarn back, slip st back onto left-hand needle, then turn and proceed as instructed. ***
Row 1: K 14(16,18), turn.
Row 2 and All Even Numbered Rows: Purl.
Row 3: K 21(23,25), turn.
Row 5: K 28(30,32), turn.
Row 7: K 35(37,39), turn.

Row 9: K 42(44,46), turn.
Continue turning in this manner, working 7 more sts in every other row until the row "k 70(72,74), turn" has been worked.
Next Row: Purl.
**** Continue in st st, inc one st at each end of the 11th row, then every 10th(12th,14th) row until there are 88(92,96) sts.
Continue until shorter edge measures 6¹/₄(6¹/₂,7¹/₂)" from beg, ending with a purl row.
Mark end of last row for back edge.
Leg Shaping:
Dec one st at each end of next row, then every 3rd row until 58(66,86) sts rem, then every 4th row until 56(60,64) sts rem.
Continue in st st until side edge measures 6(6³/₄,7³/₄)" from marker, ending with a purl row and dec 13 sts evenly across last row — 43(47,51) sts.
Change to No. 2 needles.
Work 12 rows in rib as for waist.

Bind off loosely in rib.****
LEFT LEG
Beg at waist, work as for Right Leg to ***
Row 1 and All Odd Numbered Rows: Knit.
Row 2: P 14(16,18), turn.
Row 4: P 21(23,25), turn.
Row 6: P 28(30,32), turn.
Row 8: P 35(37,39), turn.
Row 10: P 42(44,46), turn.
Continue turning in this manner, working 7 sts more in every other row until the row "p 70(72,74), turn" has been worked.
Work as for Right Leg from **** to ****, placing a marker at beg of the corresponding row, instead of at the end.

FINISHING

Sew back, front and leg seams. Thread elastic through 1st, 3rd and 5th rows of rib at waist.

LEMON SCENTED BOOTIES

TECHNIQUE: Knitting

DIRECTIONS

Using No. 3 needles, cast on 43 sts.
Row 1: (K 1, inc in next st, k 18, inc in next st) twice, k 1 — 47 sts.
Row 2 and All Even Numbered Rows: Knit.
Row 3: (K 1, inc in next st. k 20, inc in next st) twice, k 1.
Row 5: (K 1, inc in next st, k 22, inc in next st) twice, k 1.
Row 7: (K 1, inc in next st, k 24, inc in next st) twice, k 1.

Row 9: (K 1, inc in next st, k 26, inc in next st) twice, k 1.
Row 11: (K 1, inc in next st, k 28, inc in next st) twice, k 1.
Row 12: K 2 tog, k 63, k 2 tog — 65 sts. ***
Work 10 rows in st st (k 1 row, p 1 row).

SIZE

Directions are given for size 0 to 6 months.

NOTE: For slightly smaller booties use one size smaller needles and for slightly larger booties use one size larger needles than suggested to obtain the correct gauge.

MATERIALS

Fingering-Weight yarn (50 gr. ball): 1 ball; 1 pair each No. 3 knitting needles, *or any size needles to obtain gauge below*; 1 yard ¹/₄"-wide ribbon; tapestry needle.

GAUGE

On No. 3 needles in stockinette stitch (st st) — 8 sts = 1"; 11 rows = 1". Be sure to check your gauge.

Instep Shaping:.
Next Row: K 37, k 2 tog, turn.
Next Row: Sl 1, k 9, k 2 tog, turn.
Rep last row until 45 sts rem (17 sts on each side of instep).
Next Row: K 10, k 2 tog, then knit to end.
Next Row: Purl — 44 sts.
Ankle:

Next Row: K 1, * yo, k 2 tog; rep from * to last st, k 1.
Next Row: Purl, inc one st in center st — 45 sts.
Next Row: K 2, * p 1, k 1; rep from * to last st, k 1.
Next Row: K 1, * p 1, k 1; rep from * to end.
Rep last 2 rows, 3 times.

Work 14 rows garter st (k every row).
Bind off.

FINISHING

Sew foot and back seam, reversing back seam above rib. Thread ribbon through eyelet holes and tie in a bow. Fold ankle section above rib to right side.

CARRY-ALL BAG

TECHNIQUE: Sewing

This is a yellow case with plaid pockets and handles. In the picture, its extending side edges (lined with blue pockets) are folded inside along the handles to close the case. Ties and handles (cropped from the open case below) would extend from the yellow edges.

MATERIALS

☐ 1½ yards of 34"-wide pre-quilted fabric
☐ 1⅛ yards of 45"-wide checked fabric
☐ ⅝ yards of 36"-wide blue fabric
☐ ⅝ yards of 36"-wide iron-on interfacing
☐ 4 velcro dots or hammer on snaps

DIRECTIONS

(½" seams allowed)

1 Cutting: *From pre-quilted fabric,* cut two 26" x 36" pieces, for case and lining. *From checked fabric,* cut two 22" x 15" pockets, two 5" x 63" straps (pieced together as needed), two 2" x 26" bonding straps and two 1¼" x 18" ties. *From blue fabric,* cut two 26" x 8¼" pocket strips.

2 Lining: With right sides together, seam a checked binding strip to one long edge of each blue pocket strip; turn it to the inside and bind the edges. Baste each strip over a short end of the case lining, right sides

up and raw edges even. Topstitch twice through each strip to make 3 pockets.

3 Outer Pockets: Fold an outer pocket in half (to 11" x 15") with right sides together; seam it at the longest edge, then turn and press. Fold the other quilted piece (the case) in half (to 13" x 36") with wrong sides together. Place the pocket on the case, seamed edge opened and centered in both directions, and pin it to the top layer only. Turn the case over and repeat. Unfold and stitch 3 pockets edges.

4 Straps: Iron interfacing to wrong side of each strap. Fold strap in half, right sides together, and seam the long edge; turn and press. Seam 1 strap to the other at the short ends to make a loop; press seams open. Topstitch near the secured edge and repeat in rows about ⅜" apart.

5 Handles: With its joins at the bottom fold of the case, overlap the handle loop about an inch over the raw side edges of the pockets; pin. Stitch handle edges to the case from one pocket's top edge to the other.

6 Ties: Fold each tie piece in half lengthwise with wrong sides together; press. Turn the long, raw edges inside and press; stitch the folded edges together. With the raw edges even and right sides together, pin one end of a tie to the center of each long edge of the case; stitch.

7 Assembly: Pin case to lining, right sides together, pushing ties and handles inside, out of the way. Stitch the edges, leaving an opening to turn. Turn, press and slipstitch closed.

8 Closing: Open the case flat, lining side up. Turn the edges to the inside along the handles. Then fold the case in half to bring the top edges together. Reach inside and pin the two left corners together, then pin the right corners. Close to each side fold, pin the turned in edges again. Mark these 4 locations (for the fasteners) before you unpin them. Unpin. Apply the fasteners to the yellow face of the foldovers.

HOW TO USE THIS BOOK

KNITTING AND CROCHET
MATERIALS

We have suggested the weight and ply of knitting yarn for each pattern. If you prefer a knitting yarn different from the one suggested, remember to knit a test square.

ABBREVIATIONS

amt = amount
beg = beginning
ch = chain;
dc = double crochet; **dec** = decrease
inc = increase; **incl** = including
k = knit; **k 2 tog** = knit 2 together
lp = loop; **p** = purl; **pat** = pattern
psso = pass slip stitch over
rem = remaining; **rep** = repeat; **rnd** = round
sl = slip; **sp** = space; **st/s** = stitch/es
sc = single crotchet
st st = stockinette stitch
 tr = triple crochet
yo = yarn over needle

GAUGE

The correct gauge is given for each pattern. It is important to work to the correct gauge to ensure a proper fit. Read the information about gauge on page 21 before you begin knitting or crocheting.

MEASUREMENTS

The sizes of knitted garments are given from 3 months to 12 months. Remember babies of the same age can vary considerably in size, so trust your tape measure and if possible take new measurements just before you begin knitting each garment.

TO FINISH

Take care to assemble your garments neatly for a professional finish. Plain knitting usually looks best if the pieces are pressed on the wrong side, using a warm iron and a damp cloth. Some yarns and textured knitting should not be pressed, so check the pattern instructions carefully. Seams on patterned or multi-colored knitting are usually best pinned first, to ensure that patterns and colors match up. Use backstitch for joining pieces unless otherwise stated.

SEWING
PATTERNS

The patterns for most of the designs in this book are given full size on the Pull-out Pattern Sheet. Each pattern piece for a particular garment has the same outline and this is shown at the beginning of the sewing instructions. We suggest you fix the pattern sheet to a firm backing, such as cardboard. Trace the pattern pieces as you need them, using ordinary tracing paper. This way you will be able to go on using your pattern sheet for a long time. If there is a particular pattern you think you might use again and again, trace the pattern pieces onto non-woven interfacing. This will last much longer than tracing or tissue paper and can be labeled and kept without tearing or wrinkling. When tracing your pattern pieces remember to transfer all labels, instructions and markings as you go.

A few smaller patterns have been given full size. Simply trace these and you're ready to go. The pattern for the baby bears on page 71 is drawn on a grid. You will need to draw your own grid, where each square is 1 inch x 1 inch, and transfer the outline to it. To enlarge the embroidery pattern on page 61, use a photocopier at your local library or copy shop.

MATERIALS

Often a particular fabric has been suggested for a sewn item and this is the one we have pictured. Do not be limited by our choices, but experiment with your own.

KNITTING NEEDLES CONVERSION CHART						
Metric (mm)	2.25	2.75	3	3.25	3.75	4
English	13	12	11	10	9	8
US	1	2	3	4	5	6